MY GOD
IS TRUE!

MY GOD IS TRUE!

*Lessons Learned along
Cancer's Dark Road*

Paul D. Wolfe

THE BANNER OF TRUTH TRUST

THE BANNER OF TRUTH TRUST
3 Murrayfield Road, Edinburgh EH12 6EL, UK
P.O. Box 621, Carlisle, PA 17013, USA

*

© Paul D. Wolfe 2009

ISBN-13: 978 1 84871 044 3

*

Typeset in 11/15 Adobe Caslon Pro at
the Banner of Truth Trust, Edinburgh

Printed in the U.S.A. by
Versa Press, Inc.,
East Peoria, IL

TO CHRISTY,

WHO WALKED THE ROAD WITH ME,
AND WHO WALKS IT WITH ME STILL

TO HENRY, PHILIP AND CHARLOTTE,

WHO ARE DISCIPLES OF JESUS,
AND GREATLY LOVED

IN MEMORY OF
LINDA DAVIS OLSON
(1943–2007),

TO WHOM GOD
WAS FAITHFUL

Contents

Foreword

I still remember the sight. Paul Wolfe almost certainly will not. I had returned to teach for a few days at Westminster Theological Seminary in Philadelphia where Paul was a student. As I walked onto the campus on an overcast, wintry day, I saw in the distance a student purposefully making his way towards Van Til Hall for a lecture. From the distance he appeared gaunt. He raised a hand in a gesticulation of greeting. I acknowledged his wave with one of my own, all the while thinking to myself, 'I should know that man.'

Only later, in conversation with some Faculty members, did it dawn on me: it was Paul Wolfe—the bright, able student who had been receiving treatment for cancer.

Fast forward to Friday evening, May 26, 2000 and once again to Philadelphia, Pennsylvania. This time my wife and I were guests at the Seminary Graduation banquet. Unusually one student had been asked to give a word of personal testimony. Yes, Paul Wolfe. I remember turning to my wife and saying to her, 'This is the young man who has had cancer.' The graciousness of his testimony to God's faithfulness lingered long with us. Perhaps it lingers particularly in my own mind because the title I had given for the Commencement Address the following day was *'Ad Gloriam Patris:* Counsel for Graduates in the School of Christ.' The passage was John 15:1ff. Paul was a living illustration of its teaching: Abide in Christ and you will bear fruit; those who bear fruit the Father prunes that they may bear more fruit. All this is to the glory of the Father.

I am glad that now—a decade on from his treatment—Paul has been able to put his story into book form. Once you have read a few pages, and are drawn into the narrative, you will realize that these pages need no commendation from me to encourage you to read further.

With simplicity, modesty, and not a little wry humour, Paul tells the story of God's providence in his life, traces the path—where he is now able to detect it—of God's wisdom, and recounts the evidences of God's faithfulness. He does this, not in a spirit of triumphalism, but in a deep consciousness that since the Lord has employed the skill of surgeons and doctors to preserve his life, like his apostolic namesake, there must still be 'fruitful labour' for him in the purposes of his heavenly Father (*Phil.* 1:22). His ministry since then, and now this book, together constitute a down payment on that harvest.

One of the hallmarks of *My God is True!*, that makes it stand apart, is not only the engaging modesty with which the story is told, but the framework within which it has been written—a deep sense of the undergirding sovereignty and grace of God, his faithfulness, and his wisdom—a recognition that his ways are higher, deeper, and wiser than ours. While this is the story of a young man's pain, his struggles, his journey through a valley of deep darkness, it is also a story of love—Paul's love for Christ, his shared love with his wife Christy and their family circle. It is a testimony to what it means to belong to the living fellowship of Christ's people, the church.

It is almost a decade now since on Saturday morning May 27, 2000 Paul joined some eighty others who 'commenced' from Westminster Seminary. To everyone who knew his story his reception of the Master of Divinity Diploma was a particularly moving moment. But yet more moving was to think of him joining in the traditional opening hymn for the Commencement Exercises as an expression of the divinity in which he had been schooled outside of the Seminary classroom:

> How firm a foundation, you saints of the Lord,
> Is laid for your faith in His excellent Word!
> What more can He say than to you He has said—
> You, who unto Jesus for refuge have fled?
>
> Fear not, I am with you, O be not dismayed!
> For I am your God, and will still give you aid;
> I'll strengthen you, help you, and cause you to stand,
> Upheld by My righteous, omnipotent hand.
>
> When through the deep waters I call you to go,
> The rivers of woe shall not you overflow;
> For I will be with you, your troubles to bless,
> And sanctify to you your deepest distress.
>
> When through fiery trials your pathway shall lie,
> My grace all sufficient shall be your supply;
> The flame shall not hurt you: I only design
> Your dross to consume, and your gold to refine.
>
> The soul that on Jesus has leaned for repose
> I will not, I will not desert to its foes;
> That soul, though all hell should endeavour to shake,
> I'll never, no never, no never forsake.

God has been all this and more to Paul and Christy Wolfe. This is the story of their past. It is also one of a countless multitude of stories about the faithful God who holds their future. It will comfort, encourage, challenge and inspire you as you read it. You will also come to admire and feel an affection for this couple through their story. But more, I hope that through these pages—

as is certainly Paul's desire in writing them—you will come to love, trust, and admire their Lord and Saviour.

Now, please, turn from these words of introduction and read for yourself Paul Wolfe's story, *My God Is True!*

SINCLAIR B. FERGUSON
First Presbyterian Church
Columbia, SC
USA

Preface

The decision to write this book grew out of a desire to record, and thus to share with others, lessons learned during a nearly year-long battle with cancer that spanned from April of 1999 to March of 2000. Years have passed since we endured that experience, but during those years the truths that were so vividly impressed upon us in the midst of the storm have, I believe, only continued to season our souls and to shape my service as a pastor. Thus, though time has passed since those powerful first impressions, I remain eager to share what the Lord was pleased to teach.

This book is not meant to be an exhaustive treatment of the subject of suffering. The reader will be sorely disappointed if he seeks that here! Rather, it is part memoir, part teaching, with a focus on the truths that stood out in our experience.

There are few, it seems, whose lives have not been touched in some way by cancer. And of course, there is no one whose life is untouched by suffering altogether. There are all sorts of dark roads that people must travel, all shapes and sizes of sorrows to be borne. Each and every one of us must come to grips with the reality of suffering in this life, and about this the gospel of Jesus Christ has much to say. For that reason I believe there are lessons here that everyone may embrace and apply. I pray that this book will be a help in that way.

ACKNOWLEDGEMENTS

There are several people who, in different ways, contributed to making this book possible.

Drs Arthur Kobrine, Allen Mondzac and Peter Moskovitz are the skilled physicians who preserved my life. I owe them a debt that cannot be paid.

The saints of New Hope Presbyterian Church in Fairfax, Virginia, love the Word of God. For that reason (and so many others) I have loved preaching that Word to them for over twelve years. This story is, in part, their story, too. See Chapter 6.

Dave Coffin, New Hope's senior pastor, by his faithful ministry, thoughtful scholarship and welcoming friendship, has left indelible marks all over my life for which I am profoundly grateful. In short, he has shared with me his life, and thus has impacted mine. Plus, he studied in Pittsburgh, so you know he must be wise.

Sinclair Ferguson was the Barnabas behind this little book. Without his encouragement it surely would have remained *The Book I Always Wished I Had Written*. In his lectures at Westminster Seminary he taught me about God and the gospel, and by the example of his own writing and preaching he has taught me that those truths are meant to be taken from the seminary classroom and passed on to bless others. May it be so.

Most importantly, I should acknowledge my wife, Christy. The story and the lessons of this book are just as much hers as they are mine. In our wedding ceremony she looked me in the eyes and said 'in sickness and in health', and she has proven true to her word. He who finds a wife like mine finds a very good thing.

WHY THIS TITLE

Finally, let me say a word about the title of this book, *My God Is True! Lessons Learned Along Cancer's Dark Road*.

The title is taken from the words of a hymn that has come to mean a great deal to me, 'Whate'er My God Ordains Is Right.' One of the responsibilities I assumed when I began my service as a pastoral intern at New Hope Presbyterian Church in the summer of 1997 was to lead the congregation in learning some of the less familiar hymns in our hymnal. 'Whate'er My God Ordains Is Right' was one of the very first we learned together that summer. The history behind the hymn text is noteworthy: the story is told that Samuel Rodigast wrote the words in 1675 for his friend, the composer Severus Gastorius, who was suffering at the time from a serious illness.

Of course, I had no idea when I first read and taught those words just how pointedly—and wonderfully—they would address me in my own illness only a few years later. Learning that I had cancer, followed by the process of being treated for it, was in many ways a 'dark road' (see verse 1 below), but I discovered all along the way that 'my God is true' (see verse 3). I have become only more persuaded of his truthfulness and faithfulness ever since.

> Whate'er my God ordains is right:
> His holy will abideth;
> I will be still whate'er He doth;
> And follow where He guideth.
> He is my God; though dark my road,
> He holds me that I shall not fall:
> Wherefore to Him I leave it all.
>
> Whate'er my God ordains is right:
> He never will deceive me;
> He leads me by the proper path;
> I know He will not leave me.
> I take, content, what He hath sent;
> His hand can turn my griefs away,
> And patiently I wait His day.

Whate'er my God ordains is right:
Though now this cup, in drinking,
May bitter seem to my faint heart,
I take it, all unshrinking.
My God is true; each morn anew
Sweet comfort yet shall fill my heart,
And pain and sorrow shall depart.

Whate'er my God ordains is right:
Here shall my stand be taken;
Though sorrow, need, or death be mine,
Yet am I not forsaken.
My Father's care is round me there;
He holds me that I shall not fall:
And so to Him I leave it all.

SAMUEL RODIGAST (1675),
tr. CATHERINE WINKWORTH (1863,
alt. 1961)

Chronology

1998

May 23	Wedding Day
September	Back to seminary for third year of study
Fall	First symptoms

1999

January	Appointment with general practitioner
April 16	Appointment with orthopedic surgeon
April 23	Diagnosis: cancer
April 24	Surgery
April–August	Chemotherapy, Part 1
July	Pneumonia
October	Radiation
November–December	Chemotherapy, Part 2

2000

March 13	Closure: appointment in New York City

Part 1: Discovery

CHAPTER ONE

Act 1: Infamy

Just one day after the attack at Pearl Harbor, President Franklin D. Roosevelt predicted that December 7, 1941 would be 'a date which will live in infamy'. Today, of course, the same can be said of September 11, 2001. The mere mention of those dates brings to mind the loss of so many lives, as well as the anger, helplessness and fear that filled so many hearts. There is a kind of deathly chill that we feel whenever we stop and remember. Those are moments in history we are unable to forget. It is as if the dates will not let us.

For many of us there are infamous dates like that associated with events in our individual lives. Mine is April 23, 1999. On that day I was told that I had cancer. I was twenty-eight years old.

Anger. Helplessness. Fear. A deathly chill. We felt them all.

A magnetic resonance imaging (MRI) scan that morning, followed by a needle biopsy that afternoon, revealed a cancerous mass in my upper back that was pressing up against my spinal cord. That was the explanation for all of those worsening symptoms I had been experiencing, but it was certainly not the explanation we had anticipated. *A cancerous mass pressing up against my spinal cord.* That was why I had been suffering so much back pain for months. That was why I had gradually lost the use of my legs over the preceding weeks. And that was why I needed to be admitted to the George Washington University Hospital across the street from the MRI centre to begin treatment as soon as possible.

Thus began what would turn out to be the nearly year-long odyssey that was our battle against non-Hodgkin's lymphoma: surgery, followed by chemotherapy, followed by radiation, followed by more chemotherapy—combined with all of the emotional highs and lows that anyone with any experience of cancer, either as a patient or as a loving observer, knows all too well.

It was, naturally, a trying time for my wife Christy and me. But it was a learning time as well. Even along cancer's dark road, there was light. The brilliant light of God's Word guided us in our cancer pilgrimage: challenging our expectations, renewing our faith, and, above all, strengthening our hope.

Throughout this book I want to share the lessons we learned. In order to do so I will need to tell parts of our story as I go. So, I will recount our experience as a play in three acts, with lessons learned interspersed along the way.

Before the curtain rises on Act 1, let me say that I would be the first to acknowledge that our experience with cancer was not as arduous and painful as that of many others. Between the day of my diagnosis and the day when the door was finally, happily closed on the treatment process, less than one year had elapsed. But for many, the road is much longer. Also—at the risk of stating the obvious—my treatments worked. I was healed. But for many, healing never comes, the road ends in death, and loved ones are left in sorrow. I do not claim that we suffered the most. Many have travelled darker paths.

Still, I think it is true to say that a little cancer goes a long way. Though we did not suffer the most, we certainly suffered enough—enough to be given a unique opportunity (what peculiar 'opportunities' the Father gives to his children!) to consider the reality of suffering in the light of the gospel.

I should also say that though I was healed, at other times in my life some close to me were not. In God's providence our family has not been left untouched by the worst that cancer can do. In my own life the Lord has given, and the Lord has taken away. I write as one who has seen both life and death. More about that later.

WHERE IT ALL BEGAN

Though April 23, 1999 was my 'diagnosis day', we need to back up a bit to start the story. We need to back up several months to the previous fall.

In the fall of 1998 I was a student at Westminster Theological Seminary in Glenside, Pennsylvania, north of Philadelphia. I had just begun the third year of my studies, aiming to complete my degree program in four years. My goal was to become a minister. I was a member of New Hope Presbyterian Church in Fairfax, Virginia in the suburbs of Washington, D.C., and I had begun serving that congregation as a pastoral intern the year before.

Most importantly, I was newly married. Christine Olson and I had become Mr and Mrs Paul Wolfe on Memorial Day weekend of 1998. We had decided to make our home in the Northern Virginia area with the thought that I would keep up a commuting arrangement between home and school, travelling back-and-forth between Virginia and Pennsylvania by car or train and spending just a few nights away from home each week. I should also say—at the risk of making this sound like a television game-show introduction—that I enjoyed tennis, basketball, and hiking with my wife. In other words, I was, as far as I knew, a healthy twenty-eight year-old, and an active one. My forehand was my bane, but apart from that I was, on the whole, a happy man. I had every right to be. I had been given an abundance of blessings.

One particular day in the fall of 1998 stands out in my memory as the first day of this personal tale, though there did not seem to be anything momentous about that day at the time. During the fall semester I was taking only one class up at Westminster, and that freed me up to help out around the church office in various ways. So, one day that fall, New Hope's pastor, Dave Coffin, and I undertook the project of assembling bookshelves for our church office. As we put together bookshelf after bookshelf to hold the many volumes that made up our church library, the radio was on in the background broadcasting coverage of the mission of the Space Shuttle *Discovery* with astronaut John Glenn aboard. How strange, the details we remember about days so long ago. Godspeed, John Glenn.

Our story begins that day because that was the first day I felt the pain in my back that would become a near-constant companion during the months to come. Naturally, I assumed when I first noticed it that the pain was the result of the work that Dave and I had been doing all day, which included some lifting of those shelves. Nothing too heavy, to be sure, but heavy enough to make me think that I had simply strained a muscle and that taking a little ibuprofen would be the end of it.

That proved to be a vain expectation.

Taking a little ibuprofen was not the end of my pain. Neither was taking a lot of ibuprofen! The pain lingered through November, and then into December. It joined us for Thanksgiving, and stayed on for Christmas. It was on hand when we rang in the New Year, 1999. It had become the uninvited guest that would not leave! Pain-relievers did not work. Sleeping with a heating pad did not work. Sleeping some nights in the recliner in our living room did not make much of a difference, either. Inexplicably, the pain just . . . lingered.

THE SPRING SEMESTER

Finally, sometime in January, I got around to seeing a doctor. I described to her the pain I had been experiencing and told her the story of our putting together those shelves, since that seemed to be the most natural explanation. She agreed. Based upon the story I related to her, she concluded that I had likely strained a muscle in my back—nothing too serious—and that it would probably take several more weeks for the pain to dissipate. Though I did not leave her office suddenly pain-free, at least I felt that I could turn my attention to other things. There was nothing to worry about.

And as the spring semester began at Westminster, I had glorious things to occupy my attention. I had four classes on my schedule that semester, and it was, surely, one of the richest line-ups in the whole four-year curriculum. On Mondays and Wednesdays, I would be studying the book of Acts and the letters of Paul with Richard Gaffin. On Tuesdays and Thursdays, I would be learning about the saving ministry of the Holy Spirit in a course taught by Sinclair Ferguson. On Wednesday nights, I would be attending Dr Gaffin's class on the work of Christ for our salvation. And on Thursday mornings, I would round out my week with a course on the books of the Old Testament Prophets taught by Al Groves. These men were able and faithful professors who regularly provided a rich feast of instruction for their students. It was nice to know that, after the first few weeks of the semester, I would be able to sit comfortably again and take in those hours-long lectures without difficulty. It would not be too long now, surely, before this strained muscle was a thing of the past.

But, one more time, that proved to be a vain expectation. Still the pain lingered. Several weeks went by. January gave way to February. February gave way to March. It got to the point that an abundant supply of pain-relievers became an important item on my checklist of things to pack for school. And not only did the pain stick around, but now it had begun to move around. One day it was predominately on my right side; the next day, on my left. On a Tuesday it might be sharpest in my upper back; by Wednesday, around the front near my rib cage. It began to feel as if a game of Whac-a-

Mole[1] was being played out within my body: the pain goes away here today, only to pop up on the other side tomorrow!

Well then, why didn't you go back to see your doctor right away?

I did not go back to see my doctor during those months for the same reasons that many do not go to see a doctor in similar circumstances. The pain was not excruciating. There were times when it was barely noticeable. And I had reason to suspect that the cause of it was not all that serious. And, frankly, I had plenty of other things to keep me busy: textbooks to read, tests to study for, papers to write. Let's face it, going to the doctor just seems so inconvenient sometimes. So, you tell yourself, 'I'll get back to see my doctor when I've got more free time. Perhaps when spring break arrives. Or maybe when the semester is over. No hurry. No bright red warning flags here. My medical appointment can wait. After all, it's just a strained muscle. Right?'

To be clear, I do not fault that doctor I visited in January. She couched what she said to me in appropriately tentative terms. She did not make any definitive pronouncements, no guaranteed diagnoses. She offered a theory that made good sense of the symptoms I presented. For all I know a strained muscle was a part of the problem. This is not some 'let's bash the doctors' tale, charging that she and her colleagues failed me by not raising the cancer flag on day one. Far from it. In fact, if anything, I came through this whole process profoundly impressed with what doctors and nurses and researchers know, and with what they can do, and with the equipment they have at their disposal to do it. I do not fault her. Nor, I suppose, do I fault myself for coming away from that January appointment feeling somewhat reassured. There was good reason to believe that this was a relatively minor nuisance, and throughout January and February and early March I was simply too busy

---

[1] Whac-a-Mole, an arcade game in which plastic moles appear randomly from a series of holes.

with all of the commuting and studying and test-taking and paper-writing to think seriously about setting up yet another medical appointment. There would time enough for that—later.

NO TIME TO WAIT

But by late March/early April my tune was beginning to change. By then the pain had become intense enough, and disruptive enough, that Christy and I realized there would be no waiting until the end of the semester. It was time to take action. I made an appointment to see an orthopedic surgeon on April 16.

That turned out to be a very good thing, because by then yet another symptom had emerged, and this one got my attention far more than the back pain ever had. I woke up one morning to find that there was a strange tingling feeling in my toes. They felt numb, something like the way your feet feel when they have 'fallen asleep'. Over the next few days, the numbness began to climb up my legs, and then the same thing began in my arms as well. I became unsteady in my walking. I had difficulty putting on a pair of socks. Simple tasks that were previously so unnoticeable had become, well, *noticeable*, in a way that was increasingly unsettling. You should not have to focus so intently on putting on socks.

My appointment with the orthopedic surgeon on Friday, April 16, turned out to be inconclusive. I told him my months-long tale of pain and numbness. He raised the possibility that I was suffering from a herniated disk in my back that was placing pressure on my spinal cord. After all, that would have accounted for everything: the months of back pain and now this strange, new numbness in my arms and legs. An X-ray taken in his office that day did not show any signs of a herniated disk, but that still seemed to him to be a likely explanation. So, the next step would be an MRI scan. That way we could get a better picture of what was going on inside me. I was more than happy to schedule it because I was eager for resolution. After some discussion about available time slots, we settled on the morning of the following Friday, April 23.

To be honest, coming out of that appointment on April 16, I was relieved. No, not relieved of my pain and unsteadiness. None of that had disappeared. But relieved of the uncertainty. I still was not well, but at least it looked like we finally knew *why*, and there was some comfort in that. After all, the diagnosis of a herniated disk seemed to make so much sense, and at last we were taking steps in the right direction of getting this whole mess resolved. Naturally I did not relish the prospect of surgery to repair a bad back (I understood that surgery might be required), but I reasoned, 'If that's what it's going to take to get me back on the tennis court, well then, point me to the operating room. I'll gladly stumble there myself.'

I suppose the best news coming out of that day, April 16, was the simple fact that I had survived it: because of my difficulty walking, I had a rather close call with a bus as I crossed the street in Washington, D.C. on my way to the doctor's office. You see, mine is a story of preservation in more ways than one!

A FRIGHTFUL WEEK

The next seven days leading up to my MRI scan were days of rapid decline in my condition. I marvel when I remember the details of those days, all the more so because I had no idea what was actually going on within my body.

I remember spending the weekend of April 17–18 in Pittsburgh for a friend's wedding, making my way around the reception hall by shuffling along the wall, leaning on Christy, leaning on chairs. I remember returning to Westminster on Monday, April 19, for my week of classes, and realizing later that if I had felt on Monday the way I felt by Wednesday, I never would have gone. I recall awkward moments as I passed students and professors on campus: they expressed concern as they saw me shuffling about, uncomfortably, but I could barely look up from the ground to meet their gaze and reply. I remember having to stand upright for Dr Gaffin's lecture on the Doctrine of Christ that Wednesday night—standing up and taking notes at the piano in the classroom—because I could no longer bear to be seated for any length of time. I remember how two of my fellow students helped me to my car when the lecture was over.

I had a class on my schedule for the next day, Thursday, but after Dr Gaffin's lecture I decided that it was time to drive back to Virginia right away. There was no use in my staying at school another day. I was confident that my legs were still strong enough for me to drive safely, so it seemed best to leave that night.

I remember the long drive home, the all-too-familiar three hours along not-so-scenic Interstate 95. I remember how, after I got back to Virginia, the walk I had to make from my car to our apartment door felt like it lasted another three hours: with every slow, painful step up that hill, alone in the quiet darkness after midnight, I kept muttering to myself, 'One step at a time, one step at a time', until I reached our building, climbed the steps, and practically collapsed through our front door and into the bed. (No, it was not exactly a 'Hello, honey, I'm home' moment.)

I remember spending most of Thursday in bed, since that was about all I could manage. And then I remember the next day, Friday, April 23, 1999, which is where this chapter began. My parents were visiting for the weekend, and so the four of us—Mom, Dad, Christy and I—climbed into the car and headed off to the MRI centre on K Street in Washington. Actually, I did not so much climb into the car that morning as Dad picked me up and carried me to it. By that point my legs were of little use.

THE TEST RESULTS

The radiologist did not use the word 'cancer'—not at first—when he put the MRI pictures up on the board, with the light shining through from behind, and pointed out the mass next to my spinal cord that was not supposed to be there. But he began using words that ended in '-oma,' and we knew enough to understand that those are words no one wants to hear. As he continued his language became more forthright, so that there was no more need to read between the lines. I was already seated in my wheelchair when he began his report, but Christy was standing—until that moment when it dawned on her just what he was saying. Then she said she needed to sit down, too. It was not a herniated disk after all. In an instant, our world had turned upside down.

CHAPTER TWO

Who's in Charge Here?

When you find out that you have cancer, a torrent of thoughts, fears and questions runs through your mind. And objections, too. For better or for worse, there are some of those. Perhaps even *plenty* of those. You say to yourself, 'Wait a minute, I'm only twenty-eight. I'm still a month away from my first wedding anniversary. I'm still a year away from graduating from seminary. I'm supposed to become a minister. I'm supposed to enjoy tennis, basketball and hiking with my wife. Cancer isn't part of the plan. Cancer isn't what *I* would have appointed for my life had I been the one in charge!'

And then, as soon as those words cross your mind—or even pass your lips—you are confronted with the question: Well then, who *is* in charge? Who *did* appoint this for my life? And then the Bible answers.

THE PROVIDENCE OF GOD

The Lord reigns! Several of the Psalms resound with that refrain:

> The LORD reigns; he is robed in majesty; the LORD is robed; he has put on strength as his belt (*Psa.* 93:1).

> The LORD reigns, let the earth rejoice; let the many coastlands be glad! (*Psa.* 97:1).

> The LORD reigns; let the peoples tremble! He sits enthroned upon
> the cherubim; let the earth quake! (*Psa.* 99:1).

According to those passages, the Lord reigns with majesty and
strength from heaven, and his reign is rightly the cause of rever-
ence and joy here on earth. The Lord is king over creation. As we
read in Psalm 103:19, 'The LORD has established his throne in the
heavens, and his kingdom rules over all.'

Today we know even more about the Lord than what was known
about him when those Psalms were written. Today, in the light of
the redeeming work of Jesus Christ and the gracious outpouring of
the Holy Spirit, we know that the Lord who reigns is one God in
three persons, the Father, the Son and the Holy Spirit. The Triune
God of the Bible is king over creation.

And this king is no mere figurehead. The Lord is a king with
control. The traditional term for this divine control is 'providence'.
With holiness, wisdom and power, God preserves and governs all
his creatures and all that they do. Nothing that takes place is beyond the scope of his good and purposeful rule.

Consider the following passages of Scripture. Theologian Bruce
Ware has helpfully referred to these as 'spectrum texts',[1] because
they teach us that the providence of God comprehends the vast
spectrum of things that take place in the created order: events major and minor, joyful and sorrowful, public and private, no exceptions:

> Then the LORD said to him, 'Who has made man's mouth? Who
> makes him mute, or deaf, or seeing, or blind? Is it not I, the LORD?'
> (*Exod.* 4:11).

> See now that I, even I, am he, and there is no god beside me; I

---

[1] Bruce A. Ware, *God's Lesser Glory: The Diminished God of Open Theism* (Wheaton,
Illinois: Crossway Books, 2000), pp. 203–7.

kill and I make alive; I wound and I heal; and there is none that can deliver out of my hand (*Deut.* 32:39).

The LORD kills and brings to life; he brings down to Sheol and raises up. The LORD makes poor and makes rich; he brings low and he exalts (*1 Sam.* 2:6–7).

Consider the work of God: who can make straight what he has made crooked? In the day of prosperity be joyful, and in the day of adversity consider: God has made the one as well as the other, so that man may not find out anything that will be after him (*Eccles.* 7:13–14).

I am the LORD, and there is no other, besides me there is no God; I equip you, though you do not know me, that people may know, from the rising of the sun and from the west, that there is none besides me; I am the LORD, and there is no other. I form light and create darkness, I make well-being and create calamity, I am the LORD, who does all these things (*Isa.* 45:5–7).

Who has spoken and it came to pass, unless the Lord has commanded it? Is it not from the mouth of the Most High that good and bad come? (*Lam.* 3:37–38).

Is a trumpet blown in a city, and the people are not afraid? Does disaster come to a city, unless the LORD has done it? (*Amos* 3:6).

Notice the spectrum: good, bad, light, darkness, life, death, power, weakness, wounding, healing, prosperity, adversity, lowliness, exaltation, well-being, calamity, disaster. Notice the divine claim: 'I am the LORD, who does all these things' (*Isa.* 45:7). The *Heidelberg Catechism* of 1563 captures this truth well:

Question 27: What do you understand by the providence of God?

Answer: God's providence is His almighty and ever present power, whereby, as with His hand, He still upholds heaven and earth and all creatures, and so governs them that leaf and blade, rain and drought, fruitful and barren years, food and drink, health and sickness, riches and poverty, indeed, all things, come not by chance but by His fatherly hand.

Perhaps the clearest, most awe-inspiring affirmation in all of Scripture about the comprehensive providence of God is what Peter and his fellow apostles proclaimed concerning the crucifixion of God's Son, Jesus Christ. On that famous Pentecost day, Peter preached to his fellow Jews in Jerusalem, 'This Jesus, delivered up according to the definite plan and foreknowledge of God, you crucified and killed by the hands of lawless men' (*Acts* 2:23).

Then, not long after Pentecost, the apostles together confessed the same thing in prayer: 'For truly in this city there were gathered together against your holy servant Jesus, whom you anointed, both Herod and Pontius Pilate, along with the Gentiles and the peoples of Israel, to do whatever your hand and your plan had predestined to take place' (*Acts* 4:27–28).

Of course, there was no denying that Herod and Pilate and others bore responsibility, humanly speaking, for the death of Jesus. But Peter and his fellow apostles realized there was more to it than that, and they said so as they preached and prayed. They realized that the death of Jesus had taken place in fulfillment of God's plan, his *saving* plan. Here is the clearest and most comforting evidence of all that the Lord reigns!

TAKING PROVIDENCE PERSONALLY

We should also note—and here we come closer to what this truth means for the cancer patient—that the vast spectrum of providence includes the course of every human life. The Bible makes that plain, too. For example, consider these sayings from Proverbs:

The heart of man plans his way, but the LORD establishes his steps (*Prov.* 16:9).

Many are the plans in the mind of a man, but it is the purpose of the LORD that will stand (*Prov.* 19:21).

Here, too, we see that human agency is real. Man does plan. And we know that man does act in accordance with his plans. But we also see more: we see that it is the divine plan that prevails, coming to pass, not in spite of man's plans and deeds, but by God governing and directing them.

Along those same lines, Proverbs 27:1 cautions us, 'Do not boast about tomorrow, for you do not know what a day may bring.' The Apostle James takes that point from Proverbs and puts it even more pointedly:

> Come now, you who say, 'Today or tomorrow we will go into such and such a town and spend a year there and trade and make a profit'—yet you do not know what tomorrow will bring. What is your life? For you are a mist that appears for a little time and then vanishes. Instead you ought to say, 'If the Lord wills, we will live and do this or that.' As it is, you boast in your arrogance. All such boasting is evil. So whoever knows the right thing to do and fails to do it, for him it is sin (*James* 4:13–17).

Do you see how James puts the point both negatively and positively? On the one hand, he teaches that ultimately you do not direct the course of your own life. What you have in mind for today or tomorrow may or may not come to pass. He even reminds us that our very survival from day to day is not guaranteed. Human life is fragile, fleeting, vanishing like the mist. On the other hand, James teaches that *the Lord* directs the course of your life. 'If the Lord wills'. James is not requiring that we say those words or words like them every single time we express some plan for the future, but he is requiring that this recognition reside in our hearts. And if it does, then it will occasionally come out in our words. In short, we ought to take this personally: the Lord reigns—over me.

It is easier to take this truth personally when we understand what it implies—more to the point, what it does *not* imply—concerning the world in which we live. It is important to understand that God exercises his sovereignty, not by obliterating the network of cause and effect in the world but by preserving and governing that network. In other words, it is not as if cause and effect were just a phantom phenomenon, with God as the one who really does everything, taking every action, speaking every word.

No, when I tap the keys on the computer keyboard, I am the one who is tapping them, not God, and I made a genuine decision to do so. There is typing in this world under God, but God is not the typist. So, too, there is sinning in this world under his reign, but God is not the sinner. What the Bible teaches is that God rules our very real cause-and-effect world without undoing its true character.

Included in that cause-and-effect world are human decisions and actions. Also included in it are the cells of the body, some of which go bad, and developments in medical research, many of which save lives, and the actions of doctors, nurses and patients. In short, to believe in the supernatural is not to deny the existence of the natural, with all that the natural world entails, including cells and chemotherapy and human choices. It is simply to acknowledge that there is one who is *over* the natural, for that is what 'supernatural' means.

GOD'S GOOD PURPOSES

The Bible teaches not only that the Lord reigns over earthly events, but also that he is accomplishing good purposes as he does so. The classic biblical statement of this truth is found in the words of Joseph. Here is what Joseph said to his brothers about the wrongs they had once committed against him: 'As for you, you meant evil against me, but God meant it for good, to bring it about that many people should be kept alive, as they are today' (*Gen.* 50:20). Here we see many strands coming together: (1.) real human agency and responsibility (sadly, in this case, the sinful actions of Joseph's brothers); (2.) divine control bringing about those actions; and (3.) a good divine purpose for bringing them about. Joseph teaches his brothers that God had sovereignly brought about their mistreatment of him in order to fulfil his own good purpose of preserving many in the midst of famine years later. God never commits random acts. He always knows what he is doing, and why.

The Bible does shed some light—wonderful light—on what God's good purposes are, but it does not answer all of the questions we might pose. On the one hand, God shows us in his Word the big picture of his purposes, and it is a glorious picture! He is ordering all things in such a way as to lead history to its eventual conclusion, when he will put his own greatness on display both in the completion of the redemption of his people and in the execution of impeccable justice in the case of those who refused him. A wonderful and dreadful day is in store at the end of time, and God is ruling all of history, even down to its most minute details, to get us there. The Christian can take that truth quite personally: he knows that God is ordering all the events and circumstances of his own life in such a way as to lead him to his heavenly home, and to enable him to grow in godliness along the way.

On the other hand, the Bible does not provide—for that matter, it *cannot* provide—precise details as to how each and every development in our lives is contributing to the fulfilment of that grand purpose. Often those details remain a mystery to us. We may be able to observe certain outcomes that have resulted from things that have happened to us, but even then we cannot be entirely sure about the greater significance of those results. Moreover, how often have we found that the outcomes that once seemed so clear were completely overturned—sometimes just hours later?

In short, the Bible tells us just what we need to know about the purposes of God, no more, no less. We may find ourselves wondering about the details, but our constant duty is to rest content in the overarching vision that the Scriptures do reveal, a vision perfectly suited to provide that rest. History is on its way to the glory of God in the salvation of his new humanity, and the Christian can say, 'That includes me!'

This is why the Christian can confess in song, 'Whate'er my God ordains is right.' To sing those words is not to say that whatever he ordains is 'right' in the sense of being good in and of itself, and thus the source of delight in our souls. After all, many things that God ordains are instances of human wrongdoing, and fatal diseases, and natural disasters. Rather, we confess that whatever he brings to pass is 'right' in the sense of being divinely wise, perfectly suited to advance his purposes for my life, contributing in some way to the realization of history's glorious culmination. Thus, I can bless God for his wisdom in ordering my life, including its trials, and at the same time long for the day when trials will be no more. I can sing a hymn like this one even through tears, and at the same time long for the day when my tears will be forever wiped away (*Rev.* 21:4).

OBJECTIONS

It is nearly impossible to think and write about the sovereignty of God without being aware that this is a very uncomfortable idea for some people. Objections are raised.

For example, in response to the claim that God rules our very real cause-and-effect world without undoing its true character, the objection is sometimes made: But how can that be? How can cause and effect be real if God is superintending them? How does that work?

The reply is: That is no real objection; that is just a question! Merely to ask *how* a thing may be is not to have demonstrated that it *cannot* be. The *manner* of God's superintendence over creation, bringing his purposes to pass, may be beyond our capacity to explain, but that hardly leads to the conclusion that it cannot be true. And in the face of the Bible's clear teaching that it is true, we have no other option but to bow in worship and confess it, all the while admitting freely that we may not be able to explain just how this works. There is nothing contradictory here, nothing irrational. Far from it: this is the most eminently rational conviction of all, for it comes from the very Word of God. After all, God is God!

Others, uncomfortable with affirming comprehensive divine sovereignty, want to carve out exceptions to it. For example: Yes, the Lord reigns—except for the sorrowful things that happen to us. Those are beyond the scope of his control. Or: Yes, the Lord reigns—except for the decisions we make. He deliberately relinquishes his sovereignty in that area and leaves men and women as the ultimate masters of their own destinies.

But the problem with those notions (and what a wonderful, glorious 'problem' it is!) is that the Bible simply will not let us carve out such exceptions to God's providence. Remember the 'spectrum texts' we considered above.

And even apart from the explicit teaching of those passages, we have to ask: What sort of 'reign' is the Lord left with when we whittle away at his sovereignty like that? Can we really imagine the Psalmist exclaiming 'The LORD reigns!' if he thought that sorrowful circumstances and human decision-making were beyond the scope of that reign?

Let us be realistic about life in this world: is there much that happens in our lives—for that matter, is there *anything* that happens—that is not tinged by sadness (at least in measure) or related to human choices (at least indirectly)? The Lord would be left with a small kingdom indeed, if all such things were ultimately up for grabs.

Here, too, it helps to go back to the death of Jesus on the cross. Stop and think about what happened at Calvary. More to the point, stop and think about what every genuine believer thinks and feels and says about what happened there. Everyone who has true saving faith, when he is on his knees in prayer, if he thanks God for anything, thanks God that Jesus died on the cross to save his people from their sins. For what greater gift was ever given, calling forth his gratitude? Well, if he thanks God for it, then he must believe deep down that God was ultimately responsible for it. In other words, he must believe that God *brought about* the death of Jesus. After all, his 'Thank you' to God is no mere 'courtesy Thank you' by which he acknowledges the contribution of a bit-player to a drama that was out of his control.

And here is the point: he thanks God for it, knowing full well that what happened at the cross was a grievous injustice such as had never been seen in all human history.

Consider the unfathomable horror of the Holy One taking on our sin in the eyes of God. Consider the unspeakable injustice of sinful men putting to death the Living One. They crucified the Lord of glory (*1 Cor.* 2:8). And yet still, the believer, on his knees, mindful of all of that, thanks God that it happened. He is not just glad that it happened: he positively gives God the credit. Thus, deep down he must believe that God brings about sorrows as well as joys, darkness as well as light. 'I am the Lord, who does all these things.'

Not only so, but the Christian also knows full well that human decisions led to the cross—genuine, free, sinful human decisions. This he knows, for the Bible tells him so: Herod and Pontius Pilate and the Gentiles and the people of Israel all played their parts (*Acts* 4:27), making decisions and then carrying out those decisions. So why does he thank God? Why does he not just thank Herod and Pilate and leave it at that? He thanks God because he knows deep down that what those men did, they did in fulfilment of the divine plan. In other words, he knows just what Acts 2 and Acts 4 tell him in black and white. You see, by praying such prayers of gratitude, the Christian reveals what he grasps in the deepest depths of his soul, which is that the providence of God has no gaps. No holes. No exceptions. The Lord reigns over all. The Lord reigns over me.

TRUTH APPLIED

Now, what is the upshot of all of this? There are two upshots: one general, and one specific.

The general upshot is this: God is ultimately in charge of the course of my life. I am not.

The specific upshot is this: when cancer comes, it comes because God appointed it. It comes as a part of his sovereign plan for life in this cursed world, not as an exception to that plan. I may not understand *how* he brought it, but I know full well *that* he brought it.

Naturally Christy and I were not anticipating that God was going to impress these lessons upon us in the way that he did. It was a hard way. If, as the saying goes, there is nothing quite like the prospect of being hanged to focus a man's mind, then there is nothing quite like being told you have cancer to take you to the spiritual woodshed for some much-needed remedial instruction.

As Christy put it so aptly in the days just after my diagnosis, we had to face the fact that the story of our life together was not necessarily going to proceed according to the 'script' that we had authored for ourselves. Certainly the life we had envisioned before cancer came along did not feature cancer as a part of the plot. In our minds we had written out a lovely story about a man and a woman who finally make it to the altar after years of forging a sweet and solid friendship (it was almost nine years between our first meeting and our wedding day), and then share together the joys and pains of parenthood (the joys outweighing the pains, of course), until, at last, they reach their golden years surrounded by children and grandchildren who rise up and call them blessed. I think there may even have been something in the script about all of the children having perfect musical pitch, because, after all, if you are going to write your own story, why not include children who can sing like the angels?

But then came April 23, 1999, and suddenly all of that changed. Suddenly my cancer diagnosis sent the signal loud and clear that it was not *our* script we were living, but *God's*. It was our Father's providential way of saying, 'Paul and Christy, not so fast.' Suddenly we were confronted with the possibility that Christy would be a widow on the day that was to be her first wedding anniversary. It was, to be sure, an abrupt awakening, but it was no more abrupt than was necessary. Christy and I needed to be awakened—again—to the reality that God is in charge, and we are not. Our pride was wounded, but make no mistake, it was a good, merciful wounding.

It is not wrong to have aspirations for the future. On the contrary, life becomes stagnant and dreary if we do not. We *ought* to look forward. It is simply that we must hold on to those aspirations loosely, knowing that the Lord may have other plans. And, as we have already seen, it is his plan that prevails.

Understandably, we wondered (as so many do in similar circumstances) why this was happening to us. We had to remember in that moment and in so many moments later that, though we did not know the precise details of God's plan, we certainly knew his grand design: he was bringing about his own glory and our good, orchestrating every detail of our lives to that end. We knew that even my cancer he had brought to pass in order to bring us closer, somehow, to the realization of our own destinies in his plan, including our being brought more and more into conformity to the character of Christ.

In fact, that very comfort then became a calling: we knew, not only that God would bring about the realization of those purposes, but also that we had our part to play as those who must seek and find. We knew that our duty in this was just what it had always been: to trust in him, to love those around us, to seek to grow in godliness. You see, sometimes when we are suffering we get so wrapped up in wondering about the things we cannot know that we end up overlooking the things we *can* know—the precious promises of Scripture about what God's grand purposes are, the clear commands of Scripture to love God and neighbour every day, and the Lord's summons to his disciples to seek and find grace on their way to glory. The main things have not been left mysterious. The only question is, will we open our eyes and see them there, printed plainly on the pages of the Bible, and believe?

Let me be clear: we also knew that our calling was to fight this dreadful disease. The reign of God over our lives—including over our choices—does not mean that our choices are not real, and so it should never lead to passivity. There was a good fight to be fought, the fight against non-Hodgkin's lymphoma, and almost as soon as I was diagnosed we strapped on our boxing gloves. But we did so knowing that the outcome of that fight—whether the thrill of victory or the agony of defeat—was in the Lord's hands. We also knew that even if I lost the cancer-fight our heavenly Father would use that defeat to bring about the most thrilling victory of all: my entrance into the presence of my Saviour.

HERE I STAND

I know that some of my friends did not share my conviction that the Lord had brought my cancer to pass. I can recall one conversation in particular in which a dear friend made it clear that this was a claim he simply could not accept.

Setting aside for a moment the consideration that the Bible actually teaches this—that is, the comprehensive sovereignty of God—consider the question: Would we really want it any other way?

Concede that just *one* thing is out of God's control, and at that point you have opened up a Pandora's box of uncertainty and despair. If my cancer was out of his control, then how can I know how many other things are out of his control, and how can I know what they are, and whether or not he will be able to do something redemptive, something transforming, with *anything* that happens to me? When you have cancer, some want to comfort you with the notion that God had nothing to do with it. But that is cold comfort, indeed. Freezing cold.

After all, what are the alternatives? Would I really want to say that the ultimate explanation for my illness is what some rogue cells just happened to do one day? Or what the human race now justly deserves since the Fall? Or what Satan was able to bring about? Or (stepping beyond the bounds of faith altogether) what mere 'chance' brought my way? Where is the comfort in any of those claims?

Notice I said the 'ultimate' explanation. Yes, cancer does involve cells gone bad. (As I said before, the natural is real.) Yes, ours is now a cursed world. Yes, Satan is real and active. But am I left to conclude that there is no higher explanation than any of those considerations, no higher reference point, no higher purpose?

No! Take those dreadful answers and run them through the theological shredder, every last one of them. I do not want anything to do with a worldview that says that cells, or curse, or Satan is ultimate. I do not want anything to do with a pitiful, partially sovereign 'god'.

I boast in this: the trial that was my cancer, plus the trying treatments I received for it, was placed into my hands by the hand of my loving Father above. And as he placed it there he summoned me through the Scriptures to trust in him, promising that he would teach me and transform me along the way, and one day bring me into my cancer-free, sorrow-free heavenly home. The classic question when it comes to suffering is, Where is God in this? Where was God when I got cancer? Let me tell you. He was standing right in front of me, ruling my life, demanding my faith. Sovereign God! Gracious Saviour!

Once again, we need only go back to the cross. How often we need to go back there! As infamous and dreadful as cancer may be—and it is—it pales next to the darkness of the cross. See there the unfathomable horror. See there the unspeakable injustice. We Christians are quick to give God the glory for the accomplishment of our salvation by means of that most horrible event. Would we then shrink back from our deepest convictions and say in the case of cancer, 'God had nothing to do with it'? No, let us come to our spiritual senses, and bow before the Sovereign Lord.

A STRANGE WAY TO GET STARTED?

Someone might ask: Why begin here? Why make this the first lesson in your book? After all, this is an issue with which people have been wrestling from the dawn of human history, the issue of Heaven's control over earthly events. This is a truth-claim that many find controversial, even many Christians. Why not lead off with other claims, claims we can all agree on and be comforted by, and then leave this sovereignty business for a later chapter, maybe even an appendix?

The answer is that when it comes to cancer, our consideration of sovereignty cannot wait. The truth of God's good and purposeful rule cannot be consigned to an appendix. In later chapters we will take up themes like hope and joy, but there is no solid ground for hope, and there is no constant cause for joy, apart from the conviction that the one who is ordering the course of my life—the *whole* of my life, no gaps, no holes, no exceptions—is my loving heavenly Father. Armed with that conviction, trials take on a very different cast.

It is certainly true to say, 'Whate'er God ordains is right.' But the Christian can say something far sweeter: 'Whate'er *my* God ordains is right.' That is the title of the hymn. That is the Christian's song. My God. My heavenly Father. My faithful Saviour. The God who is, is a God who loves me, and I rest in his love, whatever he ordains for me. Can you sing that song?

Let us all learn to take our stand here:

The LORD reigns. Let the earth rejoice!

CHAPTER THREE

Spiritual Punctuation

A s I said at the beginning of the last chapter, when you find out that you have cancer, all sorts of fears and questions race through your mind. Naturally one of those questions is this: will God bring me healing? In other words, will all of this surgery and chemotherapy and radiation actually work? For some the question is even more pointed. They wonder, 'Has God promised to bring me healing?' In other words, can I bank on it? For that matter, just what are the promises of God? What are the things I can count on as one who believes in Jesus?

TWO CATEGORIES

It is obvious that some things in life are certain and others are uncertain. Conventional wisdom has it that the certain things are death and taxes and that practically everything else falls into the other category. There is some truth in that observation, but God's Word would inculcate an even better wisdom.

On the one hand, the Bible recognizes without embarrassment the presence of uncertainty in human experience, even in the experience of those who trust in God. In the last chapter we noted Proverbs 27:1: 'Do not boast about tomorrow, for you do not know what a day may bring'; and we saw how the Apostle James drives that point home (*James* 4:13-17).

Jesus taught this same truth. Chillingly, he taught it by telling the tale of a man who did not trust in God. He told the parable of a rich man who was also a foolish man, planning to launch a bigger-barns construction project to accommodate his vast resources—until he was caught off guard by a sudden death (*Luke* 12:16–21). That man had not come to grips with the uncertainty and frailty of life.

Several biblical stories show us this uncertainty in vivid colour. Consider the story of Job. Who could have predicted that almost instantaneously Job would be reduced from great abundance to such sorrowful want? Remember the fortunes of Babylon's King Nebuchadnezzar in Daniel 4. Who could have anticipated that he would also be so dramatically reduced, in his case driven from kingly glory to beastly humiliation . . . and then restored to his throne? Consider the mothers of Bethlehem whom we meet in Matthew 2. Who could have known that due to a fit of murderous royal rage they would be plunged into such sudden and profound sorrow?

Of course, it would be one-sided to suggest that the only surprises in life are disasters and dashed expectations. After all, some surprises are pleasant. Sometimes our lives take unexpected turns for the better. Remember the story of Joseph's brothers in Genesis 45. Who among them could have predicted that Pharaoh's prime-minister would turn out to be Joseph himself, and that he would treat them mercifully? Consider the experience of Mordecai in Esther 6. Who could have anticipated that, before the day was done, Haman would be the one leading Mordecai around the city, hailing him as the one whom the king delights to honour? Remember the story of Saul of Tarsus. Who could have forecast that such a determined opponent of the gospel would become its most influential servant?

Often when reading a novel or watching a film, some development in the plot causes us to exclaim, 'Well, I didn't see *that* coming!' We see the same thing in the Bible and in the storylines of our own lives: there is much in life, joys as well as sorrows, that cannot be predicted. We do not know what a day may bring. Uncertainty!

On the other hand, the Bible proclaims the rock-solid certainty of the promises of God. For example, God has promised that he will bestow his salvation upon all those who come to him in genuine repentance and faith, casting themselves upon his mercy revealed in Jesus Christ: 'And it shall come to pass that everyone who calls on the name of the LORD shall be saved' (*Joel* 2:32; *Rom.* 10:13). He has promised that he will abide with all those who trust in him, never withdrawing his love: 'I will never leave you nor forsake you' (*Heb.* 13:5). He has promised that he will refashion those who trust in him so that they grow in godliness, for this was his purpose even before time: God 'chose us in him before the foundation of the world, that we should be holy and blameless before him' (*Eph.* 1:4).

God has even promised that death itself will not triumph over the believer. Jesus said to Martha, the sister of Lazarus, 'I am the resurrection and the life. Whoever believes in me, though he die, yet shall he live, and everyone who lives and believes in me shall never die. Do you believe this?' (*John* 11:25–26). Resurrection means not only preservation through death, but one day—on the day when Christ returns—the presentation of a new, heavenly body fit for heavenly living: 'But our citizenship is in heaven, and from it we await a Saviour, the Lord Jesus Christ, who will transform our lowly body to be like his glorious body, by the power that enables him even to subject all things to himself' (*Phil.* 3:20–21).

Centuries before Jesus and Paul spoke those words, God had made a death-defeating promise to his Old Testament people, Israel:

But now thus says the LORD, he who created you, O Jacob, he who formed you, O Israel: 'Fear not, for I have redeemed you; I have called you by name, you are mine. When you pass through the waters, I will be with you; and through the rivers, they shall not overwhelm you; when you walk through fire you shall not be burned, and the flame shall not consume you. For I am the LORD your God, the Holy One of Israel, your Saviour' (*Isa.* 43:1–3).

The Christian rightly takes that promise personally in the face of death: when I pass through the waters—even through the flood-waters of death itself—my Saviour will not leave me nor forsake me, but he will abide with me and see me home. This marvellous promise was the inspiration behind the thrilling culmination of John Bunyan's seventeenth-century classic, *The Pilgrim's Progress*, when the pilgrim, Christian, passes through the waters before reaching the Celestial City. I find it remarkable in retrospect that I submitted a seminary paper on that very passage in Isaiah just days before I was diagnosed.

Of course, this is just a sample. So many Bible passages set forth the certainties of the gospel.

Notice that all of those promises now have a wonderful Christ-ian cast. As Paul wrote to the Corinthians concerning Christ, 'All the promises of God find their Yes in him' (*2 Cor.* 1:20). It is thanks to Jesus Christ—who he is, what he accomplished, what he is doing now, and what he will do in the end—that the believer can be certain that none of those promises will fall to the ground.

One of my favourite Bible passages expressing the faithfulness of God in keeping his promises comes from Joshua 21. Israel's victories in the land of promise are summed up this way:

Thus the LORD gave to Israel all the land that he swore to give to their fathers. And they took possession of it, and they settled there. And the LORD gave them rest on every side just as he had sworn to their fathers. Not one of all their enemies had with-stood them, for the LORD had given all their enemies into their hands. Not one word of all the good promises that the LORD had made to the house of Israel had failed; all came to pass (*Josh.* 21:43–45).

That last verse ('Not one word . . .') is one that we have taught to our children. They like to pronounce the final affirmation with great gusto: 'All came to pass!' As it was in Joshua's day, so it remains and will always remain: all of God's promises are realized.

We should also note, in order to do justice to the whole counsel of God, that the promises of the blessings of the gospel are not the only words God has sworn to fulfil. He will also keep words like these: 'It is appointed for man to die once, and after that comes judgment' (*Heb.* 9:27). 'Whoever believes in the Son has eternal life; whoever does not obey the Son shall not see life, but the wrath of God remains on him' (*John* 3:36). Death and judgment will come, and for many that judgment will mean divine wrath. These are solemn truths, to be sure, but they are no less certain, no less reliable, than the promises of salvation.

Thankfully, the Christian need not live in fear that the wrath to come will come upon him. 'There is therefore now no condemnation for those who are in Christ Jesus' (*Rom.* 8:1). He lives mindful of that coming day, and he trembles at the thought of the justice many will know—a justice he himself also deserved apart from grace—but he carries on in the confidence that in Christ he has been forgiven and covered with a record of perfect righteousness, and thus has been made ready for that day. For the believer, the outcome of his life will surely be the full flowering of eternal life with God and with his people in glory. Certainty!

PUNCTUATION REVERSED

So, life confronts us with both of these categories: the things that are uncertain and those that are certain.

Now, here is the lesson: real trouble results when we begin to confuse the two.

Think of it as a matter of 'spiritual punctuation'. On the one hand, there are some issues in life—the uncertain things—that we properly punctuate with a question mark. Will our picnic be rained out? Will I get that job for which I interviewed? Will I marry one day and have children? Will I get stuck in traffic as I drive into Washington, D.C. on Interstate 66? (Note, even *near* certainties are not *absolute* certainties!)

On the other hand, there are some matters—and here we locate the promises of God's Word—that we rightly punctuate with exclamation marks. The forgiveness of sin, the abiding presence of God, ongoing renewal in heart and mind, even preservation and home-coming when death comes! God will certainly grant all of those things to the believer!

The problem is that in our hearts we often get the punctuation reversed. We put exclamation marks where question marks belong, and vice versa.

We put exclamation marks after the uncertain things because we have managed to convince ourselves that they will certainly turn out in our favour. Even we who repudiate the sort of health-and-wealth prosperity nonsense peddled by some popular preachers may find that those lies have found a lodging in our own hearts. Even if we would never come out and say it, deep down we may be thinking, 'Surely my loving heavenly Father would never make me suffer disappointment and disaster.' This amounts to putting promises into God's mouth.

Conversely, we put question marks after the promises of the gospel because we struggle to believe that something so wonderful—and so unseen—can really be true. Or if it is true, can it really be worth all this? The ancient lie began with 'Has God really said?', and deep down we are prone to treat even his most precious promises that way.

Do you see how we tend to reverse our spiritual punctuation?

The end result is that some Christians end up living like this:

Our picnic will *certainly* be a smashing success!
Or, I will *definitely* get that job that I interviewed for!
Or, I will *certainly* be a mother of children one day!
But will God *really* abide with me in everything I go through, including death?
Or, is heaven a *real* place, and am I *truly* destined to arrive there in the end?
Or, does God *really* love me as one that he looks upon in his beloved Son?

Clearly, the results of such a punctuation reversal can be devastating. On the one hand, if I put an exclamation mark on my getting that job, believing that God has guaranteed it, but then I do not get it, I can only be left wondering, 'Is he faithless after all?' On the other hand, if I put a question mark after the promises of the gospel, doubting their truthfulness, I wake up every morning hopeless. Either way my spiritual strength is sapped: either I no longer believe that God keeps his promises, or I fail to embrace the promises he actually has pronounced in his Word.

CANCER, HEALING AND CERTAINTY

Now, here is the question: where do we put the prospect of being healed of cancer? Which category? Certain or uncertain? Exclamation mark or question mark?

This is hard for some to accept, I realize, but the answer is that it falls in the 'uncertain' category. The proper punctuation is a question mark. Instead of declaring, 'I will definitely be healed of my cancer!' the sufferer rightly asks, 'Will I be healed of my cancer?' And then, having asked, he rightly admits, 'God only knows.' This is a place where some are prone to use the wrong punctuation. They think, 'God will surely heal me!' But that is a recipe for spiritual trouble. Of course, we rightly look forward to the glorious disease-free world that Christ will inaugurate upon his return at the end of the age, and to the new bodies that will be ours in that world. That is certain! But when it comes to our physical healing now, in this world, God has made no such promise.

Some say that the Bible does give us ground to punctuate healing with an exclamation mark. They believe that God's Word provides the promise of physical restoration for those who trust in God with sufficient faith. After all, do we not read this in Psalm 103?

> Bless the LORD, O my soul, and forget not all his benefits, who forgives all your iniquity, who heals all your diseases . . . (*Psa.* 103:2–3).

And does James not say this?

> Is anyone among you sick? Let him call for the elders of the church, and let them pray over him, anointing him with oil in the name of the Lord. And the prayer of faith will save the one who is sick, and the Lord will raise him up. And if he has committed sins, he will be forgiven. Therefore, confess your sins to one another and pray for one another, that you may be healed. The prayer of a righteous person has great power as it is working (*James* 5:14–16).

And does Jesus himself not promise this?

> Whatever you ask in my name, this I will do, that the Father may be glorified in the Son. If you ask me anything in my name, I will do it (*John* 14:13–14).

Those passages sound quite certain on the subject of physical healing and answered prayer. How do we make sense of language like that?

First, we should note the stubborn fact, observable in human experience, that God does not heal all the diseases of his people, not even all the diseases of those who are strong in faith. He does not even heal all the diseases of those who believe quite firmly that he has promised to do so. That is an undeniable reality.

Second, we need to take a closer look at the three Bible passages just cited. David's observations in the opening verses in Psalm 103 resist our reading them as absolute promises. Yes, God forgives and heals and exalts and crowns and satisfies and renews. But we know—and David knew this well, too—that God does those things in his time and in his way. He does not work identically in different people's lives, nor even in any one person's life from season to season. To be sure, whatever exaltation, satisfaction and renewal we enjoy come from God, but there are times when God does not exalt, satisfy and renew, and the same is true of healing. The believer reads Psalm 103 (as he must read all of Scripture) with one eye on heaven, for our blessings in this life are but fore-tastes of the wholeness and healing that are to come.

A similar point can be made about James 5. Read the book of James from start to finish, and notice how many times he uses sweeping, unqualified language—at times, quite jarring language—even though writer and reader alike know there are qualifications and explanations that must be made in our minds. For example, consider James's unqualified language about the moral charac-ter of the rich (5:1–6), alongside the Bible's teaching that some who are wealthy are faithful (*1 Tim.* 6:17–19). Consider James's unqualified language (like that of Jesus, by the way) concerning the impropriety of swearing an oath (5:12), alongside the Bible's teaching that some oath-taking is acceptable (*2 Cor.* 1:23). On the subject of praying for the sick, James does not need to spell it out, but he knows as well as we do that prayer leads to physical heal-ing when that is part of God's plan for that person. And only then. Consider Timothy and his 'frequent ailments' (*1 Tim.* 5:23). Whatever relief Timothy may have known from day to day, God was pleased to leave him with his chronic condition.

Finally, notice that James cites the example of the prophet Elijah in the verses immediately following his discussion of healing and prayer. As James notes, Elijah prayed for rain after years of drought, and rain came in abundance. But how many faithful farmers throughout the ages have asked God for the same thing, only to find that the rain did not come? When it comes to the healing of the body and the watering of the fields, James is making no guarantees.

But what about the promise of Jesus we noted in John 14: 'If you ask me anything in my name, I will do it'? Yes, our Lord's language is sweeping, but our interpretation must not be careless. As Christians commonly recognize, praying 'in Jesus' name' does not mean tacking on those three little words at the end of every prayer as a magic formula to get God to do our bidding. Rather, it means praying to the Father as those who have aligned ourselves with Jesus' cause (which is the Father's glory, see verse 13: 'that the Father may be glorified in the Son') and who thus desire that cause to be advanced above all. But what does it look like to pray in that fashion? Jesus himself shows us. Consider the example of his prayer in the garden of Gethsemane. He laid his desires before his Father's throne ('Father, if you are willing, remove this cup from me'), but then he uttered this petition: 'Nevertheless, not my will, but yours, be done' (*Luke* 22:42).

That was how the Master prayed; surely his servants must follow his lead. Our claim to pray in Jesus' name rings hollow if we consider Jesus' *Nevertheless* to be beneath us. When the Christian prays aright he prays in the same spirit: he seeks the glory of the Father in the fulfilment of the Father's will, and to that one petition he is willing to subordinate all his other petitions. The Christian's desire for God's glory (whether spoken or unspoken in a given prayer) underlies all his requests, and that desire will be satisfied in the end. Therein lies the certainty, not in the guarantee that whatever the Christian asks God to give him, without exception, without qualification—including physical healing—will be granted.

And we should be grateful that the Bible provides no such guarantee! After all, if it were the case that the Christian could get God to give him anything he requested, the Christian would have displaced God as the sovereign director of human affairs. Where the Bible says 'the Lord reigns', we would have to erase 'the Lord' and put in its place the words, 'Insert Your Name Here.' But in that case there would be no cause to say, 'Let the earth rejoice' (*Psa.* 97:1). Consider the limitations of your own perspective as a small creature in a vast and complex universe. Then consider the confusion and folly that regularly cloud your own thinking due to sin. Do you actually think it would be a good thing if you were in charge of the world with your prayers? Can you not recall petitions you laid before the Father in the past that, in retrospect, you are grateful he did not grant, because you see now that they would have been curses instead of blessings, foolish instead of wise? With apologies to Groucho Marx ('I don't care to belong to any club that will accept me as a member'), I can say that I would not want to live in a universe that would have me—or any other creature/sinner, for that matter—as its sovereign.

Moreover, there can be only one universal sovereign, but this unqualified 'anything goes, anything's given' view of prayer puts every praying person in charge. Everyone who prays in Jesus' name is thereby elevated to the throne of the universe, possessing the power to determine what happens next. That makes for an awfully crowded throne! No, this cannot be the Bible's teaching concerning prayer, generally, and healing, specifically.

Read the Bible from cover to cover. The promise that God will certainly heal the sufferer so long as that sufferer's faith is strong enough is just not there. Not only does the Bible not provide that promise, but our experience in this cursed world mocks any claim that it does. And yet sadly many continue to punctuate the prospect of healing in this life with an exclamation mark, as if God had guaranteed it.

THE SUFFICIENCY OF SCRIPTURE

The Christian who is suffering from a serious illness faces a variety of pressures to believe that God has guaranteed his healing. Sometimes the pressure comes from those who mean well, a reality driven home to me just moments after I was diagnosed. In the MRI centre that day there were several members of the medical staff who were working on my case. When my MRI was over and we had received the radiologist's grim report, one of the medical assistants approached us and told us that the Lord had spoken to her directly and had given her a special word of assurance for me that I would be healed.

Now, I have no doubt that that woman was a genuine sister in Christ, well-intentioned in her desire to bring me comfort. But make no mistake, what she said was just about the worst thing that anyone could have said to my family and me in that moment. I derived no certainty, no comfort whatsoever from her words.

Let me explain why.

First of all, in spite of her claim that the word she had heard was a word for me to embrace, a word for my comfort, there was no way for me to know that the Lord had spoken to her. This consideration alone was enough to show that she was, sadly, confused about whatever impressions she had experienced in her mind. After all, can we even conceive of our loving heavenly Father dealing that way with his children? Would he give a word to comfort me, and yet provide no ground for me actually to believe it? Far from being a comfort, that would be cruel.

Remember Proverbs 27:1: 'Do not boast about tomorrow, for

you do not know what a day may bring.' Because there was no evidence to believe that the Lord had spoken this word, boasting like that is precisely what I would have been doing had I then gone around assuring others—and assuring myself—that I would triumph over cancer. In effect I would have been saying, 'I *do* know what my days will bring . . . even though I can't know that the Lord has provided any revelation about them.'

Secondly, had such a truth even been revealed, it would have been, frankly, useless information. I would be healed, she told us. Well, healed for how long? Five years? Five months? Five days? One day? Would I be healed on a Tuesday, only to get hit by a bus on Wednesday? In other words, I would have been left knowing practically nothing more about my future than I did before she spoke. Her word was more confounding than it was clarifying. At least Hezekiah was told fifteen years (*2 Kings* 20:6)!

It was one of those moments (and there have been others since) when I was reminded of the tremendous importance of believing in the sufficiency of Scripture—the truth that the Scriptures are sufficient to guide us, so that there is no need for personalized divine whispers to tell us what to do today and what to expect tomorrow. That is a truth with profound practical implications, and the denial of it often creates confusion and heartbreak. When Christians start listening for whispers from God that go beyond the Bible, and then believe they have actually heard some, the stage is set for profound disappointment and discouragement. How often those 'promises' end up dashed against the hard rocks of reality.

'But wait', you might say, 'it turns out she was right. You were healed.' Yes, I was healed. But no, she was not right. Had she tentatively predicted on the basis of what was known about my case that my treatments would be effective, then yes, we could look back today and say that her optimism was vindicated. But she did far more than tentatively predict. In a moment of real fear for my family and me she urged upon me a promise that I had no firm reason to embrace and claimed that that promise had come straight from my God. There was nothing right about that.

WHERE'S THE LIGHT?

I realize that at this point some readers might be thinking: 'Well, this book sure turned out to be a downer. I picked it up looking for the author to give me encouragement in the face of trials, and instead he's hammering me with all the things God has not promised. This book ought to be called *Dark, Pessimistic, Fatalistic Lessons Learned Along Cancer's Dark Road.* Where's the light?'

There are several points to make in response.

First of all, there is most definitely a place for optimism in the face of trials. There is a real power to positive thinking. And not only that, but sometimes the 'odds are good'. Sometimes the test results are promising. And when they are we ought to acknowledge that, and give thanks to God for it. By all means, keep looking to the future. God is regularly pleased to give healing to the sick, along with other earthly blessings, and in his providence we have reached an age of extraordinary medical technology and know-how by which that healing can come to pass. It would amount to ingratitude on our part to overlook those facts.

Secondly, the one who is sick is right to seek healing, even to seek it earnestly. The fact that healing is uncertain does not mean you should not go after it with whatever strength you have. We are miles away from fatalism here. By all means fight the fight, just as Christy and I did. Wage that multi-front war of research and treatment and testing and prayer.

But even allowing for the place of optimism, we have to remember that promising odds, encouraging percentages—that is not the same thing as gospel certainty, and we dare not confuse the two. We dare not confuse 'absolutely' with 'possibly'. We dare not blur the line between 'Hallelujah!' and 'Who knows?' In Hebrews our hope is described as 'a sure and steadfast anchor of the soul' (*Heb.* 6:19), and that simply cannot be said of promising odds, even the best odds. Many have learned the hard way that the promising prognosis of today can turn bleak tomorrow.

And though it is right to fight for physical survival, we have to admit that we cannot be entirely sure we will win that fight. Consider an analogy from the work of gospel ministry. Paul charges Timothy to deal patiently with opponents of the truth, allowing that 'God may perhaps grant them repentance leading to a knowledge of the truth' (*2 Tim.* 2:25). Notice the 'may perhaps'. I have heard of a sermon once preached on that text entitled, 'What the minister *must* do; What God *may* do.' We can make a similar point here about facing physical illness: 'What the patient and his doctors and nurses and friends and family *must* do; What God *may* do.' Perhaps God will bring about healing as a result of your patient endurance.

The most important answer to the charge that this book has become a pessimist's manifesto concerns the relationship between false hopes and true ones. In short, false hopes *distract*. The Bible sets before us those many glorious gospel promises—heavenly promises—but our hearts are inevitably drawn away from them insofar as we allow ourselves to bank on earthly outcomes. Exposing our misguided expectations is not pessimistic. On the contrary, it is a first step in the direction of real, biblical optimism. False hopes add up to so much spiritual debris that gets in the way of our seeing what God has truly promised. That debris has got to go.

This is analogous to the famous point that C. S. Lewis makes about pleasure in his sermon, 'The Weight of Glory'. Lewis says this:

> Indeed, if we consider the unblushing promises of reward and
> the staggering nature of the rewards promised in the Gospels,

it would seem that Our Lord finds our desires not too strong, but too weak. We are half-hearted creatures, fooling about with drink and sex and ambition when infinite joy is offered us, like an ignorant child who wants to go on making mud pies in a slum because he cannot imagine what is meant by the offer of a holiday at the sea. We are far too easily pleased.[1]

Here we can add, we are far too cheaply optimistic! We are half-hearted even in our approach to the future, allowing ourselves to become so absorbed with the prospect of earthly healing that we practically lose sight of heavenly glory. Sometimes a cancer patient who is assuming he is going to be healed needs to hear from a loved one, 'Be careful. It may be that you won't be healed.' And when such words are needed, they are loving words. To say them (gently, of course) is not to tell him that his sense of optimism is too strong, but that it is too weak. It is to tell him that he has set his sights too low, and to urge him to lift his gaze to greater things. God has not promised long life, but what he *has* promised is that he will use even death to bring believers to heaven. The lesson for the Christian is this: Stop presuming you are going to survive this illness, as if God had guaranteed it, and start rejoicing in the thought of what awaits you even if you do *not* survive it. Set your hope firmly there, in heaven, where Christ is, where your citizenship is too!

This is where the cancer patient has got to plant his flag: on the true promises of God's Word. In the moment when you learn that you have cancer, there is only one thing strong enough to hold you up. It is not the love of your wife. It is not the support of your family and your congregation. It is not the odds of your being healed—even if those odds are very good. The only reality that can truly, deeply sustain you in that moment is the hope to be found in

[1] C. S. Lewis, 'The Weight of Glory', in *The Weight of Glory and Other Addresses* (New York: Macmillan, 1980), pp. 3-4.

Jesus Christ, the one who laid down his life for his people and who then crushed death as God's resurrection pioneer.

God said to the exiles of Judah in Jeremiah's day, 'For I know the plans I have for you, declares the LORD, plans for welfare and not for evil, to give you a future and a hope' (*Jer.* 29:11), and in effect he speaks the same words to every believer. The future he has in mind for me may not involve my survival of this or that illness, but it certainly involves something far better—eternal life! Mine is a heavenly horizon.

God healed me of my cancer. But he gave no *promise* to heal me. The promises he has made point me beyond my fortunes in this life and direct my attention to the life to come. This is why I have always tried to speak about my experience in language that avoids the suggestion that God's faithfulness to me was evidenced in the fact that he healed me. The language of 'faithfulness' implies promises kept. Yes, he was faithful to me. And yes, he healed me. But those two realities did not go hand in hand. Let me put it plainly: had I died of cancer at the age of twenty-eight, leaving Christy a widow on first wedding anniversary, God would still have been what he was, and is, and will always be: the Ever Faithful One. My healing was not a promise kept; it was simply a gift God was pleased to give—though a gift he is not pleased to give in every single case.

DID GOD FAIL LINDA?

This truth becomes especially important—and especially poignant—when we remember loved ones who walked with Christ and whose battles with illness ended in death. This book is dedicated to the memory of Linda Davis Olson. Linda was my wife Christy's mother, and on April 20, 2007 Linda died after a valiant campaign against cancer that lasted over two years. Anyone who knew her knew that Linda was strong in her faith in Jesus Christ.

So here is the question: Did God fail Linda? Did it turn out that he did not have a future for her after all? God did not heal Linda. So then, did he abandon her?

No, No . . . a thousand times No! God was perfectly faithful to Linda. He kept every last promise he had ever made with her in mind. We sang, 'Great Is Thy Faithfulness', surrounding her bed as she lay dying in her home, and then we sang it again at her memorial service after she was gone. And it was the perfect hymn to sing.

After all, what had God promised her? To heal her of her cancer? No. But something far better. He had promised to stand by her as a loving heavenly Father in the face of her greatest fears, and then to use death to bring her to her eternal home. That is what he had promised, and that is precisely what he did. Her God was true! All came to pass! As I write and as you read, she is in glory right now, basking in the blessedness of heaven, praising God for his faithfulness far more earnestly than she ever did when she was here on earth. Sometimes I struggle to confess that 'Whate'er my God ordains is right'. But Linda does not struggle with that truth any more.

THE SUM OF THE MATTER

The sum of the matter is this: Trust in God's written word— no more, no less.

No more. That means, do not put promises into God's mouth. Do not start adding assurances to the Bible that the Author did not put there. Acknowledge the question marks in life, and do not try to erase them.

No less. That means, do not live in practical denial of the glorious things our Father has promised to do for his children. Marvel at the exclamation marks of the gospel, and let them dwell richly in the depths of your heart.

Part 2: Endurance

CHAPTER FOUR

Act 2: Treatment

A t the end of Act 1 in our story, we had reached the ominous moment in the infamous day when the radiologist told us what the MRI pictures told him. The rest of that day was a fearful, colourless blur. More tests followed. CAT scan. Sonogram. Needle biopsy. Needle biopsy *repeated.* (If at first you do not get a sufficient tissue sample, try, try again.) And then we waited for the results of that biopsy. And then we got those results back from the lab. And then, at the end of that very long day, we finally left the radiology centre and drove across K Street to be admitted to the George Washington University Hospital. Treatment had to start as soon as possible.

Someone pointed out I had been wheeled through the same emergency room doors where President Ronald Reagan was rushed after he was shot in 1981. We were not much in the mood for presidential trivia. What a Washington moment.

NON-HODGKIN'S LYMPHOMA

At this point a brief word about non-Hodgkin's lymphoma may be helpful. Cancer of any kind boils down to cells behaving badly: reproducing out of control, refusing to die when they are supposed to, invading and shutting down vital organs. Lymphoma is a type of cancer in which the badly-behaving cells are those of the body's lymph system, a network of vessels and tissue that is an important part of the anti-immune system. Because that network runs throughout the entire body lymphoma can show up practically anywhere, and spread almost anywhere, too. Over thirty variations of lymphoma have been identified, including a subfamily of the disease that was first described by a man named Thomas Hodgkin in the nineteenth century (thus the distinction between Hodgkin's disease and non-Hodgkin's lymphoma). How ironic, that a bodily system meant to fight disease becomes the locus of a potentially fatal disease.

We discovered from the beginning that getting cancer means having to learn things about the body that you never knew before—that you never had any reason to know before. In my case the learning curve was especially steep. Had you asked me in March of 1999 what I knew about non-Hodgkin's lymphoma, I may very well have guessed it was a type of cancer first researched by a man named Non Hodgkin.

SURGERY

Even before I was wheeled into that hospital emergency room a team of doctors was being assembled to take responsibility for my care. Because of the precise location of my tumour I needed an extensive team. (As it is with real estate, so it is with tumours: 'location, location, location.') First, I needed an orthopedic surgeon, because the operation to remove my tumour would involve dealing with the bones of my spinal column. Second, I needed a neurosurgeon, because the tumour was right next to my spinal cord (that is, the bundle of nerves that runs within the spinal column). And third, like every cancer patient, I needed an oncologist. Thankfully, the team of doctors that came together that day turned out to be a kind of Washington 'dream team'. We even learned that the doctor who was to serve as my neurosurgeon was the one who had operated on President Reagan's press secretary, James Brady, after Brady was shot during that same assassination attempt.

There was some question at first as to what the strategy for my care should be. Should they operate first and only then proceed to things like chemotherapy and radiation? Or should they start with radiation in order to reduce the size of the tumour and then operate as a second step? After some back-and-forth between the members of my team the decision was made to operate first. In retrospect that turned out to be a wise decision. Our neurosurgeon informed us later that, had they not operated as soon as they did, I might have been left permanently paralysed. My tumour was placing so much pressure on the nerves of my spinal cord, and had already done so much damage to them, that I might have passed a point of no recovery if they had not operated quickly to remove it.

The surgery took place first thing Saturday morning, April 24. I do not recall much about that day, largely because I spent most of it in that happy, happy place where anaesthetic drugs can take you. In fact, I was probably the happiest member of our family that day. Drug-induced ignorance was bliss.

But the memory of that day is not a total loss. I remember friends and family members coming to visit as soon as they got the news. I remember making and taking a few phone calls in spite of the fact that I was not entirely aware of what I was hearing and saying. And I remember—of all things—getting the hiccups as I lay in bed recovering in my post-operative room. Getting the hiccups just a few hours after major surgery on your back is not advised. That was *not* a happy place.

EIGHT LONG DAYS

I ended up spending just over a full week in the hospital. I was not released until Friday, April 30. Those eight days were unlike anything I had ever experienced. Before that week I did not have much experience with hospitals. Well, apparently this was going to be my opportunity to catch up—with a vengeance.

Each day was a blur of tests and doctor visits and nurse visits and hospital assistant visits and, alas, hospital food. Also, because George Washington is what is sometimes described as a 'teaching hospital,' often when a doctor visited my room he led a cadre of students in his train. I had gone from being a student to being studied!

Others visited, too—so many that we started to keep a record. It is remarkable for me now, all these years later, to go back and read the many names on that list. And the phone calls kept coming. And the cards poured in. Christy and I both felt like we were being carried along by many who loved us.

Perhaps most loving was the friend who visited me in the hospital and brought me a four-pack of a fine European beer. Not surprisingly, my nurses took a rather dim view of his love. Enjoying that gift would have to wait for another time. I had been placed on one of those strict 'no European beer' diets that some cancer patients must patiently endure.

CHEMOTHERAPY

It was also during that first week in the hospital that I received my first round of chemotherapy.

That word alone—'chemotherapy'—has the power to provoke all sorts of emotions, especially for anyone who has ever been on the receiving end. That is because almost everybody knows what chemotherapy is for and what it can do to you. The crack has been made, 'Cancer's not so bad. It's the medicine that kills you,' and that observation does have a ring of truth. Still, for all of its side effects, chemotherapy does often have the primary effect of saving your life, and it did that for me. I thank God for those noxious chemicals.

The first time they give you chemotherapy they have to keep a pretty close eye on you because they cannot be sure how your body will react. After a while, as the summer went on, chemotherapy became strangely routine. But that first time we all held our breath a bit as we watched the drugs make their way down through my intravenous tube and into my bloodstream. Thankfully, the drugs did not throw me for too much of a loop. The whole thing was over in just a few hours.

Throughout the summer there would be five more rounds of this particular form of chemotherapy, the last administered in late August, each of them involving the same four drugs they gave me that day in the hospital. They spaced out my rounds so that there were approximately three weeks between each pair. Cycles of chemotherapy: that became the strange rhythm of our summer months.

The only interruption to that rhythm came in July thanks to my coming down with pneumonia. One of the side effects of chemotherapy is that it weakens your body's immune system and leaves you more susceptible to a variety of maladies, pneumonia included. Our doctors had prepared us for this possibility. So, instead of being surprised that I got it, we were actually a bit surprised that I had made it all the way to mid-July without any such complications. Pneumonia meant being back in the hospital, which was not exactly heartening, but there was some comfort in knowing that I was getting the round-the-clock care I needed. Plus, this hospital stay lasted less than a week.

To be precise, it was a matter of two hospital stays, one right after the other. I was initially released on a Saturday, only to realize late that same night that I was not as well as we had thought and that I needed to go right back. We returned to the emergency room about twenty-four hours after being discharged. As wonderful as the care was that we received there, a hospital emergency room is not a place where you want to become a familiar face. There is no way around it: cancer takes you on a roller coaster ride.

Having said that, though I am certainly not pro-pneumonia, I did not mind the reprieve from chemotherapy that my pneumonia gave me. Instead of three weeks between rounds at that point, we waited a full five weeks. We needed to make sure my body was ready for those drugs again. Eventually it was, and when it was, the rhythm resumed.

And speaking of chemotherapy . . .

MY NEW LOOK

On a Tuesday, I went bald.

At least, I think it was a Tuesday. It may have been a Wednesday. I do not recall precisely. In any case, one day in May I woke up with hair, and by lunchtime of that same day I had no hair. We had been told to expect it any day as a side effect of my chemotherapy, so I was not caught off guard.

The reason I went bald so quickly, in a matter of mere hours, is that once I realized that the first tuft of hair had come out I took action to *make* myself bald. I became positively proactive about my baldness. I was not going to sit around and just let it happen, slowly, here and there, for days. When I found those first strands in the palm of my hand I decided to get to work. Armed with a razor, a towel and a mirror, I made it happen. It did not take too long to finish the job once I got started.

Some men look good bald. Yul Brynner. Telly Savalas. Michael Jordan. Then there are the rest of us. We wear hats. At least, at first I wore hats. My friends gave me some great hats. I was well supplied. But after a while I gave up on covering up. It may not have been pretty, this new side that I was showing the world (my top side), but life without hair and hats was so wonderfully low-maintenance. And when you are a cancer patient, minimizing maintenance is a priority. For the rest of the summer, my head was naked, and I was not ashamed.

And speaking of side effects . . .

STEROIDS

As with many cancer patients, my chemotherapy regimen entailed a cocktail of drugs. Mine included four drugs commonly referred to by the acronym CHOP, each of those letters standing for one of the four medicines. The 'P' in CHOP stands for the steroid Prednisone. In addition I was also taking a steroid called Decadron. These are not steroids that have the effect of bulking you up (which is what usually comes to mind when people hear that 's'-word), but anti-inflammatory drugs commonly used as anti-cancer medications.

The downside is that even these drugs can have pernicious side effects. I found myself affected mentally, physically and emotionally, and without question those effects were among the most difficult aspects of my whole experience.

What was most remarkable was how the steroids had my mind racing. Every minute felt like it was packed with about three minutes' worth of thoughts and questions and ideas. My brain was on hyper-drive. At first I thought, 'Wow, this is great! Think of all the reading I'll do! Think of all the biblical and theological problems I'll solve!' All of a sudden I was a seminarian on the juice, and I had great expectations. 'Oh, the many home runs I'll hit!'

That initial enthusiasm lasted for a few weeks. Yes, I did some reading. I memorized some Scripture passages. I recorded some thoughts. I felt productive. For a while.

But after those first few weeks I began to feel mentally exhausted from all of that mind-racing. I started reaching less for books and more for the remote control, because *Antiques Roadshow* and 'M*A*S*H' reruns were about all that my head could handle. I grew tired of every minute feeling like three, and I found myself longing to return to normal speed. I got to the point that I just wanted to rest my head, but, maddeningly, I found that I could not. Borrowing from Ecclesiastes: there is a time to be intense, and a time to chill. But my mind never seemed to shift out of intense.

Christy and I would regularly go to bed at around 11:00, and if I managed to sleep until 3:00 that was a pretty good night. There were some nights when I would wake up closer to 1:00, and that would be the end of my sleep. That meant approximately five hours to myself until Christy woke up, which, according to my three-to-one ratio, felt more like fifteen hours. Those were *long* nights. I would spend them watching television, eating, reading, eating, writing, eating, thinking, eating.

Did I mention eating?

That was another side effect of my steroids: my appetite shot off the charts. I became hungry with a hunger I had never known, a hunger that was nearly impossible to satisfy, like some frightful beast in a bad horror movie: *The Seminarian That Just Kept Eating.* I would stand at the refrigerator and look over the foods on the shelves, wondering what might be fair game for me to eat. And usually my conclusion was, 'Hey, it's *all* fair game!' All the old rules about what foods are appropriate to eat at what time of day—those rules were out. I would start eating at 3:00 A.M. or so and finally stop, not because I felt full—I seldom did—but simply because I felt it would not be right to keep going.

And because my appetite shot off the charts, so did my weight. Well, not exactly off the charts. I was not breaking any scales. But I was not a terribly weighty fellow to begin with, and when you add quite a few pounds to a fellow like that, it shows. One of my doctors referred to it as a chemotherapy side effect known as 'truncal obesity'. I called it other things. Add to that the bulky back brace I had to strap on later in the summer, and eventually I crossed the line into 'truncal monstrosity'. It is no wonder that I barely recognize myself when I look back at old photos from that summer. I can only imagine how I must have frightened the little children in our neighborhood. ('Mommy, here comes that big strange man with the cane and the unsightly bald head and the look of unrelenting intensity!')

To top it off—and Christy could tell you more about this than I could—I was liable to mood swings. When somebody is thrown off mentally and emotionally as I was, it is a good bet that those closest to him will bear the brunt of it. And Christy did. It is one thing to have to watch your husband undergo treatment for cancer. It is another thing to have to watch and, at the same time, wonder just who your husband is going to be from one day to the next, even from one hour to the next. I could be tender. I could be irritable. I could be overwhelmed by minor things. I could be oblivious about major things. I could be weepy about dumb things. And I could be all of those in the course of about fifteen minutes.

So, there you have it. Cravings. Weight gain. Mood swings. Plus, I received epidurals. I had it all. We joked that I would be one of few ministers who could say to pregnant women in the congregation, 'I feel your pain. I've been there.' Of course, now that Christy has given birth to three children—including twins—I do not crack that joke quite so much any more. I have not been there.

And speaking of life-changing side effects . . .

MATTERS OF TASTE

When you are being treated for a deadly disease, confronted with the reality of your own mortality, wondering how many days you have left, it seems almost inappropriate to be bothered by the fact that your food does not taste good any more. But it did not (taste good). And I was (bothered).

I first noticed it during that first week in the hospital in April, but it became most clear the Friday that I was discharged. Naturally we viewed that as a day to celebrate. And just as naturally (from my vantage point, at least) celebrating meant ordering pizza when we got home. You see, I am a big fan of pizza. And after a week in the hospital—eating hospital food—I was especially eager to order pizza first thing when we got home. And so we did. And then we waited for the pizza to come. And then the pizza came. And then I took my first bite.

I do not know quite how to describe it except to say that it was a lot like the way they describe it in those *Chemo and You* pamphlets they give you in the hospital, which contain warnings like this: 'Among the side effects of chemotherapy you may find that your food comes to have a slight metallic taste.'

Great. Metal pizza. As if lymphoma were not enough.

And it was not just pizza. It was everything. Or, almost everything. I did manage to find a few foods that did not seem to have that strange taste. In fact, that became something of a summerlong campaign: The Great Quest to Find Foods That Taste Like What They're Supposed to Taste Like. The first breakthrough was, of all things, diet root beer. (It was, admittedly, a desperate campaign.) And then there was cheese con queso dip. And then there was rice pudding. I ate a lot of rice pudding.

It does seem strange to get so wrapped up with things like food when you are effectively fighting for your life, but, on second thought, is that really so strange after all? God designed us in such a way that our lives are made up of so many little things, and our sense of well-being is powerfully affected by our fortunes in those mundane matters. That is just part of being human. And when you add to that being human with cancer, you become downright eager to pay attention to something else, anything else, besides chemo and CAT scans and the constant weight of uncertainty. Food becomes something normal to think about.

TESTING, TESTING

But you can only avoid thinking about your disease for so long. Eventually it finds a way to command your attention again. Like whenever you have to go in for yet another medical test.

If you have ever had cancer, or if you have ever been close to someone who did, you know that one of the most emotionally draining aspects of the whole experience is the seemingly non-stop cycle of tests and test results. Each one of those tests is designed in its own way to reveal what is going on in your body, and so each time you have to prepare yourself for what that revelation is going to be. The news might be good; the news might be neutral; the news might be very bad.

The list reads like a category on a television game show. ('I'll take medical acronyms for $200.') MRI: Magnetic Resonance Imaging. CAT: Computerized Axial Tomography. PET: Positron Emission Tomography. MUGA: Multigated Acquisition. (That is a scan of the heart). Plus tests of your bone density, and tests of your bone marrow. There are tests that require them to put substances into your body beforehand (like the radioactive substance, gallium), and then there are tests that require you to empty your body beforehand. And in preparation for a lot of those tests you have to drink things. Nasty things. Things you would not order in a restaurant. They try to make them palatable by adding things like artificial banana flavour, but there are some wonders that even modern science cannot accomplish.

But as it is with chemotherapy, so it is with all those tests: I thank God for them. Thank God that we have the technology today—truly marvellous technology—to see so clearly what is going on in the body in order to treat disease more effectively. We were also grateful that the first series of tests I underwent after getting out of the hospital in April revealed that my lymphoma had not spread beyond that one location near my spine. So, we were dealing with a relatively confined cancer. That was the good news.

NERVE DAMAGE

But we were dealing with a tumour that was confined to a most regrettable location. That was the bad news. And that was also, increasingly, the source of my frustration throughout the spring, then summer, then fall.

Though I knew there was cancer in my body, a disease that would kill me if we did not kill it first with this barrage of treatments, I may have been even more absorbed from the beginning with the question of the recovery of my mobility. For months that growing tumour had been placing pressure against my spinal cord, doing neurological damage. That is why, by the time I was wheeled in for surgery that April Saturday, I could barely walk. And practically from the very first moment after I awoke from that surgery I wanted some doctor to tell me and to tell me with certainty: when will I play tennis again? That was very near the forefront my mind. 'Healing? Survival? Sure, I want to survive. But doctor, let's cut to the chase: will I survive as someone who can run?'

I left the hospital in April with a cane and with unrealistic expectations about how long I would need it. I had gotten it into my head (in spite of my doctors' more cautious estimations) that my surgery would have me back up and mobile in no time, just like before. But with the passing of days, and then weeks, and then months, it became clear that if my nerves were going to rebound, they were going to take their own sweet time. And even that was an 'if'. My doctors could not make any guarantees about how much of my mobility I would ever regain.

But I was obsessed with it. I wanted so badly just to run again. I monitored my own movements moment by moment like a hawk, searching desperately for any indication, any hint, that my nerves were waking up and that my mobility was coming back. That very desperation only added to my emotional exhaustion. Those who knew better kept telling me to be patient about my progress—to continue with my exercises, to keep swimming regularly in the pool in our neighbourhood, that sort of thing—but I found patience to be a hard virtue. Christy and I got a lot of good parking spaces that summer thanks to the temporary handicapped parking permit that was now dangling from our rear view mirror, but make no mistake: I wanted nothing more than to be done with that permit and with all that it represented. I felt the same way about my cane.

I began having dreams—very realistic dreams—in which I was back on the tennis court, running around freely, playing joyously, just like before. Except in my dreams, all of my forehands landed *in*! And then I would wake up and realize that it was just a dream, and I would weep. I had those dreams over and over and over again. It got to the point that in the very narrative of my dreams I would suspect I was dreaming, and therefore tell myself not to get my hopes up, only to wake up and feel hopes dashed once again. My disappointment was new every morning.

It was certainly a strange experience for a twenty-eight year old, having to learn again how to walk. That is not one of those learning processes you anticipate ever having to revisit. But there I was, not too far from age thirty, having to stop and think again about what walking involves. (Just when do you lift the back foot? And when is it supposed to land again? And when is my knee supposed to bend? I mean, it is supposed to bend, right?) I remember sitting on a bench and watching people go by—watching them *walk* by—and trying to figure out from their movements how the whole thing was supposed to work. What a moment it would have been had I actually approached one of them and said, 'I'm sorry, but could you go back and do that again? I'd really like to see what you do with your feet.'

In a matter of weeks, I had gone from studying theology to studying an activity that young children go about with ease—and I was failing at it.

RADIATION

In the meantime, the fight against cancer itself raged on. When we were done with summer chemotherapy it was time to turn our attention to radiation. Fall is supposed to be the time when you turn your attention to college football, but we had already gotten used to the idea that the seasons would have a different feel in 1999. October has always been my favourite month, but in 1999 October was my own personal Radiation Awareness Month.

We had gotten good news in September: a battery of tests indicated that there was little cancer left in my body, if any. The chemotherapy had done its good work. But radiation was still called for. After all, there might have been some cancer left, and even if there was not, radiation would decrease the likelihood that my cancer would ever come back.

In my experience undergoing radiation treatment was not so much painful as it was inconvenient. Unlike chemotherapy, which I received once every three weeks, radiation would be administered almost daily: this was to be a Monday-through-Friday routine for four straight weeks. So, each morning of the workweek I would make my way back to the hospital in Washington, D.C., park, walk to the radiology wing, wait for my turn, get treated, and leave. Day after day after day. The irony was that the procedure itself—the actual radiation 'zap'—lasted for all of about thirty seconds. It seemed to me that whenever you brave Washington traffic you should spend at least sixty seconds on your actual errand! In any case, I was grateful that those radiation treatments did not have any nasty side effects. On the whole it was a painless experience, more an investment of time than a medical ordeal. I realize that radiation is not so painless for others.

CHEMOTHERAPY, PART II

So, by the middle of November, we had endured three major phases of treatment: surgery in April, followed by chemotherapy throughout the summer, followed by radiation in the fall. But we were not quite finished.

The last step in my anti-cancer regimen was a series of chemotherapy injections that I received throughout November and December. Unlike the chemotherapy of the summer months, which was administered intravenously (that is, into the veins), this series of treatments at the end of the year would be 'intrathecal' (which means, administered into the region around the spinal cord, called the theca). My oncologist wanted to take every appropriate measure to make sure that there were no cancer cells lurking in that part of my body. Unfortunately, getting anti-cancer medicine into the region around the spinal cord involves having a very long needle inserted into your back. Fortunately, I could not see it happening. All I could see was the wall I was staring at as I lay on my side and waited for the whole process to be over. Christy could have seen it happening had she been in the room, but our doctor had seen enough caring spouses faint at the sight of that very long needle being inserted into the back that he had learned to ask visitors to leave the room. She would come back in when it was over.

When that series of treatments began we were not sure just how many injections it would involve. Eight? Six? We ended up doing only five. That was largely attributable to the fact that my body did not handle them well. Injections like those are notorious for causing bad headaches, and I suffered plenty of those. And worse. I even spent the day before Thanksgiving back in the hospital undergoing a minor procedure designed to lessen the side effects. In light of the fact that I was reacting so badly to those injections, and since they were only precautionary to begin with (there was no urgent need for them), the decision was made to call it quits after the fifth one.

We did not know it at the time, but that last dose of intrathecal chemotherapy was the last treatment of any sort that I would have to undergo for my cancer. Had we known, no doubt we would have danced! But at the time it felt like the days of dancing were still a long way off. It was just too soon. Too soon to know if there might be further precautionary treatments in store. Too soon to know if my cancer was about to make a quick comeback. Sometimes it does that.

CHAPTER FIVE

Heart Tests

A s I noted in the last chapter, a cancer patient undergoes a variety of medical tests as he is being treated for his disease, tests that reveal the condition of his body. Among those tests are some that take pictures of his heart for all to see. At the same time, he is undergoing spiritual heart tests, too. The Bible refers to the soul of a man as his 'heart', and suffering reveals his condition in that sense as well. In particular, he finds himself constantly confronted with this heart-question: What is the source of your deepest joy?

HABAKKUK'S RESOLUTION

The Old Testament prophet Habakkuk shows us the source of true joy in the glorious conclusion of the book that bears his name. At the beginning of the book Habakkuk is not joyful but profoundly perplexed. He does not understand the Lord's dealings with his rebellious people. Not only does the Lord seem to be tolerating their rebellion, but then the Lord's solution—which is to use the armies of Babylon to chasten them—does not sound like much of a solution at all. As the prophecy continues, however, the Lord provides an assurance of his faithfulness that Habakkuk takes to heart, so that the once-perplexed prophet is finally found trusting in his God. Here is his concluding confession:

> Though the fig tree should not blossom, nor fruit be on the vines, the produce of the olive fail and the fields yield no food,

the flock be cut off from the fold and there be no herd in the stalls, [18] yet I will rejoice in the LORD; I will take joy in the God of my salvation. [19] GOD, the Lord, is my strength; he makes my feet like the deer's; he makes me tread on my high places (*Hab.* 3:17–19).

What a remarkable confession that is! The grim scenario that Habakkuk describes in the opening verse is no litany of minor misfortunes. These are matters of life and death. And yet even as he contemplates that scenario he is resolved to rejoice. What can account for such a disposition? Notice that in verses 18–19, Habakkuk himself provides the explanation. We can see five reasons for his rejoicing even in the face of such dire circumstances.

First, Habakkuk knew God as Israel's covenant God. He refers to God twice in this passage using the covenant name 'Yahweh,' which is the name behind the all-capitalized 'LORD' (verse 18) and 'GOD' (verse 19) in our English Bibles. No doubt Habakkuk grasped the gracious significance of that name. Beginning with Abraham, God had condescended to establish a unique relationship between himself and the people of Israel. As Moses reminded them, 'The LORD your God has chosen you to be a people for his treasured possession, out of all the peoples who are on the face of the earth' (*Deut.* 7:6). The name 'Yahweh' became the name by which God's chosen people regularly referred to him and personally addressed him in prayer. God himself had revealed the name for that purpose. Out of all the peoples who were on the face of the earth, Israel alone knew the one true God by name!

Further, it was a binding relationship. This was no mere temporary alliance, no mere passing friendship. God had bound himself to Abraham and his descendants with promises that could never be broken, including the promise that those descendants would one day form a vast nation and that God would show himself to be their Saviour. God even swore in a dramatic covenant-ratification ceremony that he would prove faithful to those promises (see *Gen.* 15). As a result, Israel could know (borrowing words from Jesus) that no one would be able to snatch them out of Yahweh's hand. They could know (borrowing words from Paul) that nothing would be able to separate them from Yahweh's love. That did not mean God would be unwilling to chasten his people, even reducing them to a remnant in comparison to their former glory, if that was what they needed. Indeed, that is precisely what he assured Habakkuk he would do by bringing the Babylonians against them. Rather, God's covenant with his people meant that even the justly-deserved disasters he dealt them would serve in some way to advance the cause of their redemption as a people, culminating in the ministry of the Messiah. Every faithful Israelite could take those truths personally, Habakkuk included. Even if earthly calamities came to pass, so that he and his neighbours were left with nothing, Habakkuk could know that he would still have the Lord and that the Lord would still have him. No wonder he was resolved to rejoice!

Second, Habakkuk knew the Lord as the God of his salvation (verse 18). The Lord had kept his promise, time and time again, to deliver the people of Israel from their enemies around them. More importantly—more personally—he had shown himself to be the Saviour of every sinner who trusted in him, granting forgiveness in this life as well as the hope of an eternal life to come.

Admittedly, the Old Testament does not teach us about the realities of personal salvation as clearly as the New Testament does. This is precisely what we would expect, since those gracious realities only fully came to light with the coming of Christ and with the subsequent outpouring of the Holy Spirit. Still, Hebrews 11 reminds us that those who trusted in the Lord before the time of Christ did so with the prospect of eternal life in view: Abraham and those who trusted in Yahweh as he did are numbered among those who 'desire a better country, that is, a heavenly one' (*Heb.* 11:16). Habakkuk and his fellow 'pre-Christ Christians' may not have grasped the truths of personal salvation as fully as we do today, but their personal faith and hope were real all the same. When Habakkuk called the Lord 'the God of my salvation', he understood, though dimly, that he had been saved from the judgment of Israel's just and holy God, and saved for eternal life with him and his people. As he contemplated the prospect of no fruit, no food and no flocks (verse 17), no doubt he longed for a future day in this life when those natural blessings would be restored. But he must have looked ultimately to that future eternal day when the ups and downs of Israel's temporal fortunes would finally give way to an eternity of settled-ness and certainty and peace. Habakkuk's horizon was, above all, a heavenly one.

Third, Habakkuk knew the Lord as the sovereign ruler over all. This, too, is reflected in the way that Habakkuk addresses him. Behind the title 'Lord' in the phrase 'GOD, the Lord' in verse 19 is the Hebrew word *Adonai,* a title by which those in authority were often addressed. Fittingly, *Adonai* became a title by which Israel regularly addressed God himself, for he possesses ultimate authority. Though the nations around them also gave titles of lordship to their gods—for example, the title 'Baal' meant 'lord,' and that is how many of the gods of the Canaanites were named—only Israel's God actually deserved to be addressed in that way. Yahweh was the Living God who ruled the whole of creation. As we saw before, Israel gladly confessed, 'The LORD reigns!' For that reason Habakkuk could know that if the trials he describes in verse 17 came to pass, it was none other than the Lord himself who had brought them to pass. Nothing was beyond the scope of his all-wise providence on behalf of his people.

Fourth, the Lord was the source of Habakkuk's spiritual strength: 'GOD, the Lord, is my strength' (verse 19). Anyone who knows himself well must admit that he lacks the strength, left to himself, to flourish in the midst of trials. The one who trusts in the Lord acknowledges this freely: 'On my own, I am weak.' But thankfully he can also acknowledge that the Almighty does not leave his people to their weakness. He transforms them. He makes the weak strong. Paul learned this when Christ assured him, 'My grace is sufficient for you, for my power is made perfect in weakness.' Paul could say, 'Therefore I will boast all the more gladly of my weaknesses, so that the power of Christ may rest upon me . . . For when I am weak, then I am strong' (*2 Cor.* 12:9–10). Isaiah confessed this, too:

> Have you not known? Have you not heard? The LORD is the everlasting God, the Creator of the ends of the earth. He does not faint or grow weary; his understanding is unsearchable. He gives power to the faint, and to him who has no might he increases strength. Even youths shall faint and be weary, and young men shall fall exhausted; but they who wait for the LORD shall renew their strength; they shall mount up with wings like eagles; they shall run and not be weary; they shall walk and not faint (*Isa.* 40:28–31).

Fifth, the Lord had made Habakkuk spiritually sure-footed: 'he makes my feet like the deer's; he makes me tread on my high places' (verse 19). We all know, as Habakkuk did, that the terrain of life can be treacherous, especially in the midst of difficult circumstances. Yet the believer is never totally lost. He always has a sense—deep-down, and faint though it may be—of knowing where to step, because he always knows that he can turn to his ever-present Father and cast all his cares upon him. He knows that trusting in Christ is the way to go, and that this way leads to his eternal destination. Yes, at times he struggles as he makes his way, and yet underlying those struggles is a settled sense that the

Lord is guiding by the light of his Word and providence.

Five reasons for rejoicing: covenant, salvation, sovereignty, strength and sure-footedness.

What stands out about Habakkuk's confession is that he found his deepest joy in the Lord himself. All five reasons, taken together, boil down to that one reason. Though the Lord gives many good things to his people, the most precious gift he gives them is a relationship with himself. 'This is eternal life', said Jesus, 'that they know you the only true God, and Jesus Christ whom you have sent' (*John* 17:3). All other goods pale in comparison with that one. All other blessings are rightly understood only in relationship to that greatest of blessings.

THREE MORE WITNESSES

Habakkuk is not alone in the Scriptures in showing us the substance of true joy. Consider three other witnesses.

First, listen to David in Psalm 27:

> One thing have I asked of the LORD, that will I seek after: that I may dwell in the house of the LORD all the days of my life, to gaze upon the beauty of the LORD and to inquire in his temple (*Psa.* 27:4).

David longed to gaze upon the beauty of the Lord, to grow in his knowledge of him and of his ways. Now, we know from David's other Psalms, as well as from the account of his life in the books of Samuel, that David asked many things of the Lord. How can he say here in Psalm 27 that he asked just this one thing? He must mean that this was the one request that trumped all others. This was his deepest desire. Knowing the Lord was David's deepest joy.

Second, listen to Asaph in Psalm 73:

> Whom have I in heaven but you? And there is nothing on earth

that I desire besides you. My flesh and my heart may fail, but God is the strength of my heart and my portion forever (*Psa. 73:25-26*).

Did Asaph truly mean that there was nothing on earth that he desired beside the Lord? No doubt there were earthly goods that he desired, for it is part of being human to desire earthly happiness. He must mean that knowing the Lord was his chief desire. All other blessings that Asaph might have wanted, however luminous they might have appeared when viewed in isolation, looked dim next to the brilliance of the glory of God. We find the same to be true today. Knowing the Lord becomes that pearl of great price for which we would be willing to give up all other treasures.

Third, listen to Paul as he addresses the Philippians:

But whatever gain I had, I counted as loss for the sake of Christ. Indeed, I count everything as loss because of the surpassing worth of knowing Christ Jesus my Lord. For his sake I have suffered the loss of all things and count them as rubbish, in order that I may gain Christ ... (*Phil.* 3:7–8).

See Paul's single-mindedness. He deemed knowing Christ Jesus his Lord to be of surpassing worth, so much so that all other things could be counted as loss and rubbish.

Thus we see that these other biblical witnesses—David, Asaph and Paul—add their 'Amen' to the truth we have gleaned from Habakkuk. Those three men testify along with Habakkuk that one's deepest joy is rightly found in the knowledge of the Lord, and in him alone.

JOY ON TRIAL

Habakkuk's confession would encourage us even if we only had verses 18 and 19, in which he describes his joy in his Saviour. But we have more than those two verses: we also have verse 17 before them, the one in which he anticipates such sweeping devastation and loss. That is what makes his confession especially striking. Against the dark backdrop of verse 17, his resolution to rejoice shines all the more brightly.

This reminds us of an important truth about suffering: suffering has a way of putting your joy on trial. I mean 'trial' in both senses: your heart is pressured (tried) by difficult circumstances, and then the way you respond is entered as 'Exhibit A' before a courtroom packed with observers—family, friends, colleagues, neighbours, doctors, nurses and others—who witness firsthand where your joy truly lies.

In the first chapter of his first letter, Peter exults in the salvation that belongs to those who belong to Jesus Christ, and he is confident that his readers exult with him. He writes:

> In this you rejoice, though now for a little while, if necessary, you have been grieved by various trials, so that the tested genuineness of your faith—more precious than gold that perishes though it is tested by fire—may be found to result in praise and glory and honour at the revelation of Jesus Christ. Though you have not seen him, you love him. Though you do not now see him, you believe in him and rejoice with joy that is inexpressible and filled with glory, obtaining the outcome of your faith, the salvation of your souls (*1 Pet.* 1:6–9).

Notice that Peter is addressing those whose joy had been put on trial. Though they had been 'grieved by various trials', they still rejoiced in their great salvation. In particular, they did so as those who loved Christ, their great Saviour. Theirs was an inexpressible and glorious joy because of their relationship with him, even though they had never seen him with their physical eyes. They walked by faith, not by sight. Notice this: their various trials had not made them joyful. Rather, their trials had simply brought out their joy for all to see. As we read this passage we are those who have packed the courtroom. We are left rejoicing, too, when Peter enters the evidence. How wonderful to see how his readers' hearts were oriented!

One who understood this truth well was the seventeenth-century Scottish pastor Samuel Rutherford. Throughout his life Rutherford carried on a remarkable ministry of letter-writing to members of the congregation he served, as well as to other friends and family members, using pen and post to encourage them with the truths of the gospel. Today we have over three hundred of Rutherford's letters preserved.

On September 14, 1634, Rutherford wrote to a woman whose husband had died just two days before. Rutherford knew from personal experience that the death of one's spouse ranks high among sorrows (his first wife had died in 1630), and he acknowledged this in his letter to her. He wrote, 'I must out of some experience say, the mourning for the husband of your youth be, by God's own mouth, the heaviest worldly sorrow (*Joel* 1:8).'[1] He knew that hers was a grief not to be treated lightly or dismissed. Yet he also knew that the Lord was at work to bring about good. In particular, Rutherford trusted that the loss of her husband would serve as a heart test that would show others where her deepest joy was to be found. He urged her, in the midst of her sorrow, to

> let God, and men, and angels now see what is in you. The Lord hath pierced the vessel; it will be known whether there be in it wine or water. Let your faith and patience be seen, that it may be known your only beloved, first and last, hath been Christ.[2]

Those are stirring and challenging words. He wanted this wom-

---

[1] Samuel Rutherford, *Letters of Samuel Rutherford* (Edinburgh: Banner of Truth, 1984), p. 100.
[2] Rutherford, *Letters*, p. 100.

an to appreciate the fact that her joy was now on trial as a result of her husband's death. It was her heart that was now being tested and revealed. God and men and angels were watching. Of course, God already knew what was in her heart, but men and angels needed to see it, and in any case the all-knowing God was still worthy of a faithful display. And Rutherford was confident that she would make just such a display. He knew her well enough to know that the results of her test would be heartening. He wrote,

> I am now expecting to see, and that with joy and comfort, that which I hoped of you since I knew you fully, even that ye have laid such strength upon the Holy One of Israel, that ye defy troubles, and that your soul is a castle that may be besieged, but cannot be taken.[3]

As it was with those who read the Apostle Peter's letter, so it was with this woman who read Rutherford's letter: her loss had not made her joyful; rather, it would have the effect of revealing the joy in Christ that she already had.

Understanding joy against the backdrop of trials in this way helps us to grasp what true, biblical joy is. Put negatively, rejoicing in the Lord is not a matter of denying the value of earthly blessings—whether possessions, people, opportunities, successes—and deadening ourselves to any desire we might feel for them. Not at all. As I have said, it is part of being human to desire earthly happiness. It is right to take delight in the blessings of this life and to feel real sadness when they are suddenly taken away, or never known at all.

It is a caricature of Christianity to suggest that true piety amounts to resisting the temptation to enjoy anything, as if we ought to live in a constant state of gloom simply because we know that things fall apart and that people let us down. When we confess with Asaph that 'there is nothing on earth that I desire besides

[3] Rutherford, *Letters*, p. 101.

you', we are not saying, 'Lord, there is nothing on earth that I desire besides you because, well, as far as I can see, there's nothing really all that desirable here anyway.' That would be faint praise, indeed! No, we rejoice in the Lord because he is so much more valuable—infinitely more valuable—than even the most wonderful of natural blessings. That is why, in this life, we sometimes find ourselves rejoicing in the Lord through our tears. Rejoicing in him runs deeper than the various emotions we experience—proper emotions—about our fortunes in this world. In short, it is right to feel satisfaction and sorrow concerning the gain and loss of temporal blessings, all the while counting Christ to be the blessing that far outweighs them all.

TRUTH APPLIED

These truths concerning joy were some of the lessons Christy and I had to learn as we made our way down the cancer road. We underwent heart tests at many times and in many ways. We regularly found ourselves confronted with that piercing question, 'Paul and Christy, what is the source of your deepest joy?' If, as I noted before, medical tests are often known by acronyms (MRI, CAT, PET), perhaps we should coin one here. Let us call it a 'DJI' scan: Deepest Joy Imaging.

We had to learn that we could not find our deepest joy in our health, since good health had proved to be so fleeting. Neither could I find it in the ability to play the sports I loved, since I could no longer be sure that I would ever walk unaided, let alone run around those courts again.

We also had to learn that we could not find our highest joy in the prospect of professional reward. I say that 'we' had to learn that. Really, it was Christy who was given a unique opportunity to learn that lesson for the both of us. At the time of my illness she was working on Capitol Hill, serving on the staff of a committee of the U. S. House of Representatives. She had recently played a behind-the-scenes part in getting a piece of legislation written and passed by the Congress, which meant that she had received an invitation to be in attendance in the White House Rose Garden when the President signed that bill into law. A White House ceremony! Now that was something to look forward to. The ceremony was set to take place on Thursday, April 29. Little did she know when she received and accepted the invitation that by the time April 29 rolled around, her husband would be in the hospital, having been diagnosed with cancer just days before. When you turn to the April 29 page in her 1999 calendar, you find two things written in Christy's hand. At the top is written 'signing ceremony'—a reference to the White House event she had been anticipating. Directly beneath is written 'Paul's 1st chemo'—that captures what the day turned out to be. On April 29 I was still in the hospital, receiving my first round of chemotherapy.

It was a striking instance of how suffering forces you to see things in a new light. What had once appeared on the horizon as a grand event—full of excitement, evoking a sense of professional satisfaction and reward—had suddenly become overshadowed with fear. Christy had to sit there in the White House Rose Garden during the ceremony knowing that less than a mile away her husband was receiving drugs that might or might not save his life. She left that White House ceremony in tears and rushed back to the hospital as soon as she could. Whatever temptation Christy might have felt before that day to make professional satisfaction the be-all and end-all of life had suffered a stinging blow.

In short, we had to learn that we could not find our deepest joy in any earthly good. You see, the Lord had given us such a good life before cancer came along. Though we had never embraced a health-and-wealth prosperity gospel, the Lord had been pleased to give us able bodies and an adequate bank account. More valuable than that, he had brought us together in marriage. Plus, remember that we had the rest of our very good life all scripted out in our minds! My diagnosis presented us with the prospect that nearly everything, present and future, would be taken away.

There were many times throughout our experience when we stood at a spiritual crossroads. In the face of this or that fear, or struggle, or setback, could we say with Habakkuk, 'I will rejoice in the Lord'? Could we confess with David that the one thing we desired most deeply was 'to gaze upon the beauty of the Lord'? Could we pronounce with Asaph, 'There is nothing on earth that I desire besides you'? Could we affirm with Paul, 'I count everything as loss because of the surpassing worth of knowing Christ Jesus my Lord'? Or would our response run something like this? 'No, Lord, this is too much. No more joy. Not for now. Joy is on hold for now. We'll get back to joy when we get back the things these current events have taken from us. Until then, we're calling time-out.'

How foolish, how faithless it would have been for us to respond that way! Put joy on hold? Only if the gospel had been put on hold—which, of course, it had not, and would never be. Christ was never, in any moment—not even in the darkest of our moments— anything less than infinitely worthy of all our delight, and to think that we were inseparably united with him through the faith he himself had worked in our hearts. Could we possibly conceive of calling a time-out on joy?

Even in hymn-singing I found my heart tested in this way. One of my favourite hymns is 'Praise to the Lord, the Almighty!' One particular line in that hymn that almost always arrests me when I sing it is the question in verse 2:

> Hast thou not seen
> How thy desires e'er have been
> Granted in what He ordaineth?

I vividly recall singing that hymn—including that question—with the congregation one Sunday evening not too many weeks after I was diagnosed. That is quite a question to be asked in a moment like that!

As I sang that question it was as if the seventeenth-century hymn-writer was reaching down through the ages to interrogate me. And my brothers and sisters in the congregation, singing around me, were joining in the interrogation. 'You there, the one with cancer, you tell us: Have you not seen that your desires have been satisfied in the things that God has brought to pass in your life? Tell us, sir, what is your answer?'

Apart from faith in Christ my answer to that question in that moment may very well have been a resounding, gut-wrenching No! 'No, I have not seen that. Do you want to know what I see right now? Let me tell you: I see chemotherapy and disability and death. That's what I see. And no, I wouldn't call that the granting of my desires. But thanks for asking.'

That might have been my answer apart from faith in Christ. But thankfully, by God's grace, it was precisely through the prism of faith that I was able to read the question, so that the answer I gave in my heart was very different. 'Yes, I have seen that. I have seen that the Lord has given me nothing less than the gift of knowing him, which is the one thing I desire most. Plus, I have seen that he has promised the coming of a day when the trials of this life will have vanished like so many strange dreams. So, yes, I have seen that my deepest longings have been satisfied in what God has ordained for my life, for he has ordained that I should be his child and heir.'

And so, in the end, I could conclude by saying, 'Thanks for asking', after all. You see, a spiritual interrogation like that one is a blessing. It is one thing to be told, 'God has granted you the one gift that matters most by far.' It is another thing to be asked—so that you have to provide the answer—'What do you see? Can you not confess that God has blessed you?' In that moment it is as if the whole world is watching and waiting to hear your reply, and the silence is deafening and dramatic until you provide it.

SEEKING JOY

Although there is no question but that Christians have abundant cause for joy, for many it is a question how to proceed in search of joy. Just what is the part we have to play in this? We know that the Scriptures command us to be joyful. Paul writes to the Philippians, 'Rejoice in the Lord always; again I will say, Rejoice' (*Phil.* 4:4). James writes, 'Count it all joy, my brothers, when you meet trials of various kinds, for you know that the testing of your faith produces steadfastness' (*James* 1:2–3). In passages like those, joy is treated as an imperative.

But this may strike us as strange, even impossible. How can I suddenly make myself feel joy? Surely we cannot turn on an emotional switch in response to a command. Is it not impossible to manufacture genuine spiritual affections in a moment?

The answer is twofold. First, though genuine affections are not a matter of sheer will power, we can willingly direct our minds to meditate upon the truths that make for joy. The pattern here (as it is with many aspects of the Christian life) is mind-work leading to heart-results. In short, we feel genuine joy when our minds turn to consider the reasons we have to be joyful. And directing our minds in that way is something we can do. We can, in any moment, stop and consider what Christ has done for us and the gospel promises that stand upon that foundation. We can, in any moment, bring to mind the reasons for rejoicing that Habakkuk shows us. Covenant. Salvation. Sovereignty. Strength. Sure-footedness. And when we do, with the blessing of the Spirit, real joy is the result. The question is, Will we take the time to do that mind-work, and do it well?

Thankfully, we can take up that work trusting in the grace of God. That is, we can deliberately turn our attention to the joy-making truths of the gospel knowing that our God already rejoices over us in Christ ('He will rejoice over you with gladness'—*Zeph.* 3:17), that he has already begun the renovating work of making us joyful in reply ('You believe in [Christ] and rejoice with joy that is inexpressible and filled with glory'—*1 Pet.* 1:8), and that he will not let that work go unfinished ('He who began a good work in you will bring it to completion at the day of Jesus Christ'—*Phil.* 1:6). We seek joy not as those who are left to their own meagre resources to find some way to find a feeling, and then desperately to try to make that feeling last. Rather, we seek it as those enveloped by the grace of God. The grace of God will triumph in the end.

Second, the command to rejoice challenges us to lift our gaze and look down the life-long road of Christian discipleship. Not only can I direct my mind to the things that make for joy—and do that now—but also I can press on in my steady seeking of the Lord, day-by-day, year-by-year, with the aim that I grow in joyfulness over time. Just as the cancer patient undergoes periodic medical tests to track his progress over the long haul, so the Christian takes regular doses of the gospel medicines that the Great Physician has prescribed (the Word and sacraments, prayer and fellowship) with the aim that his joy-condition improve with the passing of time. And it does take time.

In God's providence it may be that your own sense of joy is on trial as you read this. Perhaps you find yourself in the midst of circumstances right now in which your own heart is being sorely tested. Whatever our precise circumstances—ease or difficulty, plenty or want—this is a good test for all of us to take, the Deepest Joy Imaging scan. To what degree do the testimonies of men like Habakkuk, David, Asaph and Paul resonate within your own soul? Whether you find that your joy is abundant, or has slowed to a trickle, stop and think again about the reasons for rejoicing that the Bible itself sets before you. Lift your gaze and look down the long road of discipleship and seek that gradual increase in joyfulness that the Lord is pleased to grant his children. If you look far enough down that road, you can even see the unmixed joy of heaven at the end.

Christian, 'Hast thou not seen how thy desires e'er have been granted in what He ordaineth?' Now, you answer. And think carefully and faithfully before you do.

CHAPTER SIX

You'll Never Walk Alone

'**M**isery loves company.' So the saying goes. A better saying would be this: those who face miserable circumstances love the company of those who will stand by them and share their burdens. From the outset of our ordeal Christy and I had many who stood with us. First and foremost, we had each other. If truth be told, she was the one who was doing most of the standing . . . both literally and figuratively.

It would be difficult to exaggerate the importance of family and church family in the life of the one whose joy is on trial.

THE HUMAN COMMUNITY
In the beginning, man was made a social creature:

> Then God said, 'Let us make man in our image, after our likeness. And let them have dominion over the fish of the sea and over the birds of the heavens and over the livestock and over all the earth and over every creeping thing that creeps on the earth.' So God created man in his own image, in the image of God he created him; male and female he created them. And God blessed them. And God said to them, 'Be fruitful and multiply and fill the earth and subdue it and have dominion over the fish of the sea and over the birds of the heavens and over every living thing that moves on the earth' (*Gen.* 1:26–28).

Both in the act of creating man, and in the divine word that preceded it, we see that God never intended there would be just one human being on the earth, living a solitary life, working and playing and worshipping all by himself. No, God's plan was that there should be a human community. The first pair, Adam and Eve, were commanded to be fruitful and to multiply, so that eventually there would be many on earth who would love God and their neighbour.

The account in Genesis 2 reinforces this:

> Then the LORD God said, 'It is not good that the man should be alone; I will make him a helper fit for him.' . . . So the LORD God caused a deep sleep to fall upon the man, and while he slept took one of his ribs and closed up its place with flesh. And the rib that the LORD God had taken from the man he made into a woman and brought her to the man. Then the man said, 'This at last is bone of my bones and flesh of my flesh; she shall be called Woman, because she was taken out of Man' (*Gen.* 2:18, 21–23).

Here especially we see that man was not made to live in isolation. Marriage was meant to be the sweetest society in the midst of a larger human society. Husband and wife would enjoy the most intimate fellowship human beings could know. They would pursue together the calling to make the most of the world God had given them, as well as the responsibility to raise children who would do the same.

Sadly, sin poisoned everything. In Genesis 3 we read of Adam and Eve's disobedience to their Maker, and in time the fallout of that Fall would be bitter indeed. Instead of living in a harmonious society, man would now wage war against his fellow man. Instead of companionship and fidelity in marriage, husband and wife would now suffer alienation and betrayal. Instead of children being raised for worship and service, parents would now pass on their own self-centredness, producing unloving children in their own image.

Happily, the Fall in the garden and its repercussions for human relations were not the end of the story. God did not abandon the human race. Instead he set in motion his eternal plan to redeem for himself a new humanity out of the old. Nor did he obliterate the institution of the family in that redemptive plan. Instead he intervened to restore and advance it. In short, God's gracious intention was that there should be love on earth after all; harmony, fidelity, friendship.

In the fullness of time the church emerged as the earthly representation of that new humanity. Prior to Christ's coming, the church was the people of Israel. Following his coming and work, the church became the assembly of all those, everywhere, who are the disciples of Jesus Christ. According to the New Testament, this new society is, in fact, a new spiritual family. As Paul puts it, the church is 'the household of God' (*1 Tim.* 3:15). Christians know God as their heavenly Father. They relate to one another as brothers and sisters. They even look to Jesus Christ as the pre-eminent brother in the family. He who was and is the eternal Son of God became a man just like us—except for sin—in order to live and die and be raised to life for us. He did so in order that those united with him by faith might enter into God's family by adoption. The good news of the gospel is that by grace the Father of Jesus Christ is our Father too!

As those who are now spiritually related in this way, members of the church are called to love and support one another:

> Let love be genuine. Abhor what is evil; hold fast to what is good. Love one another with brotherly affection. Outdo one another in showing honour. Do not be slothful in zeal, be fervent in spirit, serve the Lord. Rejoice in hope, be patient in tribula-

tion, be constant in prayer. Contribute to the needs of the saints
and seek to show hospitality (*Rom.* 12:9–13).

As fellow Christians we ought to serve one another as Paul describes.
Also, we ought to let others serve us. We do not often think of
it as a duty to let others help us when we are truly in need, but is
that not an implication of the Golden Rule? 'So whatever you wish
that others would do to you, do also to them' (*Matt.* 7:12). Is this
not how you want to be treated by others: do you not want them
to accept your offers of kindness in times of need, instead of turning you away with a not-terribly-truthful, 'Don't worry about it;
I'm okay'? When we receive new members into the congregation
I serve, we regularly encourage the rest of the body to 'allow them
a place of service in your lives'. Is that not the way it should be?
Sometimes your Christian duty is to let others serve you. Humility
works both ways; it is a matter of giving and receiving.

Not only is the church as a whole meant to be a transformed
society in the world, but Christian families are designed to be
microcosms of that society—'little churches' in which the same
virtues of love and forgiveness, honour and encouragement are put
on practical display. The last word of the Old Testament predicted
that the ministry of the forerunner of the Messiah would be one of
restoring love and honour in families: 'And he will turn the hearts
of fathers to their children and the hearts of children to their
fathers' (*Mal.* 4:6). That promise has come true in every Christian
home where parents and children, wives and husbands, rightly relate to each other under God. Marriage, in particular, has been
given new life thanks to the gospel, husbands and wives relating to
each other with a love that mirrors the bond between Christ and
his church (*Eph.* 5:22–33). United in marriage and united with
Christ they make their way heavenward together as fellow heirs of
the grace of life (*1 Pet.* 3:7). Love restored.

Not surprisingly, love within the family of God stands out all the more remarkably in circumstances of trial and suffering. Christians step up when fellow Christians have fallen down into difficulty, and perform practical deeds of brotherly care. Paul charged the Galatians to 'Bear one another's burdens, and so fulfil the law of Christ' (*Gal.* 6:2). This is the law of our Saviour, that we should come to the aid of our brothers and sisters in the Lord, helping them carry the burdens that weigh them down. And we are to do this not merely as a matter of form, but with a heart full of sympathy. Paul wrote to the Christians in Rome, 'Rejoice with those who rejoice, weep with those who weep' (*Rom.* 12:15). He also taught the Corinthians: 'If one member suffers, all suffer together; if one member is honoured, all rejoice together' (*1 Cor.* 12:26).

The book of Proverbs reminds us that 'A friend loves at all times, and a brother is born for adversity' (*Prov.* 17:17). In some cases the bond of friendship is even closer than that of natural brotherhood: 'A man of many companions may come to ruin, but there is a friend who sticks closer than a brother' (*Prov.* 18:24). The tie that binds fellow church members is not natural but super-natural friendship. That is, we belong to one another not as those who have earthly interests in common, but as those who share a common bond with Christ.

Whatever our natural similarities and differences may be (physical appearances, political convictions, employment, hobbies, etc.), ultimately we are bound to one another as those who are bound to Christ. That is a tie that trumps all others, and it is for that reason members of the church ought to stand with one another and care for each other. We do so, ultimately, for Jesus' sake, regarding one another as those who are greatly loved by him.

IN SICKNESS AND IN HEALTH

All of these biblical truths concerning family and church family hit home when you are suffering from a serious illness: then you appreciate all the more those who lovingly surround you.

I have already noted several dates that stand out as I reflect upon our story. Here is one more: May 23, 1998. Our wedding day.

And what a glorious day it was!

It did not start out particularly glorious—certainly not weather-wise. But just in time, the skies cleared and the sun shone. At the high point of the ceremony, in the midst of those wonderful 'repeat after me' vows, I promised to Christy that I would stand by her in sickness and in health, and then she made the same promise to me. And she meant it. And so did I.

But little did we know.

The day that I was diagnosed was exactly eleven months after our wedding day. 'In sickness and in health' suddenly took on new significance.

When our first anniversary finally rolled around one month later, it turned out to be memorable in ways we could not have anticipated. The fact that there was a dramatic thunderstorm that evening only made it all the more memorable! Making our way to the fine restaurant where we had made our reservations, we did our best to push fears aside and to be grateful for the time we had been given as husband and wife. Unable to drive because of the useless-ness of my legs, I rode along on the passenger side, seat reclined so that I could rest, watching the lightning light up the sky. It was another one of those moments when we felt a jarring discrepancy between the expectations we had once entertained and the reality that had come to pass.

Even from a culinary perspective it was bitter-sweet. There we were, on our first wedding anniversary, in a fine restaurant . . . and I suspected that none of those exquisite dishes on the menu would taste right to me, not with my twisted sense of taste. Cursed chemotherapy! (I can only imagine the reaction of the waiter had

I ordered the diet root beer with a bowl of rice pudding.) Christy and I certainly had not imagined that we would be celebrating the first year of our life together under such circumstances. But at least we still did have that—*life* together—and for that we were grateful.

As the months went by Christy learned that it is not just the one who has cancer who bears new burdens. The spouse does too. In one way her burdens were heavier, because hers were largely unseen. I was the one who was bald and bigger and hobbled, but Christy looked no different. What others could not see were the fears she had to endure, along with the extra tasks that she had to shoulder every day because of my condition. To top it off, as I mentioned before, she had to deal with me in all of the moodiness brought on by my medication. She stood by me in sickness and in health . . . and in (my) distorted personality too.

As a result, Christy is much more sensitive now to what the spouse is going through when someone gets sick. Several times, when we have learned about a friend or family member being diagnosed with cancer, she has sought out and encouraged the spouse: 'Don't be surprised by the emotional burdens you'll be bearing. Don't be surprised when this person you love all but disappears personality-wise due to his chemotherapy. Don't be shy about accepting others' offers of assistance. For that matter, don't be shy about asking for help without waiting for those offers to be made.'

Our experience with cancer had the effect of vindicating some good counsel we had received before we got engaged. Back then, when we were wondering about whether to get married, we found ourselves stymied by a host of questions concerning the future: where would we live, where might I serve as a pastor, did Christy even want to be the wife of a pastor in the first place?

A wise friend pointed out that, though it was perfectly appropriate for us to consider the future and to anticipate what life might entail, in the final analysis there was just one question we had to answer: did we love each other? That is, did we love each other enough to come together as husband and wife and thus set out to share whatever God's providence would bring? Were we willing to make our two lives into one shared life with all of its shared uncertainty?

Remember that Proverb: 'Many are the plans in the mind of a man, but it is the purpose of the LORD that will stand' (*Prov.* 19:21). When two people get married they may have all sorts of plans, but the fundamental issue is this: will they travel together the path of life come what may, in joy and in sorrow? They cannot know in advance what and when those joys and sorrows will be. They may find that most of their plans come to pass. Or they may find that one of them has cancer eleven months after their wedding day . . . if not sooner. And then everything changes. Before we got engaged Christy was wondering about becoming the wife of a pastor. What she did not know—indeed, what she could not know—was that she would first have to become the wife of a cancer patient.

During my service as a pastor I have had the opportunity to counsel several couples in anticipation of their wedding day, and then to serve as the minister in their ceremony. Now I get to lead others through those same 'repeat-after-me's. As they make their promises I tell each one to say 'in sickness and in health', and they do so. I know now more fully than I did on our wedding day what that promise means. In my pre-marital instruction I make a point to say so, and to tell them why.

GREATLY LOVED

Christy was not the only one who was standing by me in sickness and in health. We had a whole congregation, and an army of friends and family beyond, who were standing by both of us.

I will not even attempt to make a full record of the ways in which others generously cared for Christy and me during our experience. If I did this chapter would quickly resemble one of those poorly thought-out Academy Award acceptance speeches in which the recipient starts out naming the names of those who deserve to be thanked, only to get cut off by the band when he has not even made it past his second-grade teacher 'who taught me that I could spell if I just tried hard enough'! There were too many who served us, and in too many ways, for me to mention them all. If you have ever gone through an experience like ours, you know what I mean.

Still, I will mention two examples of the service we received. First, a fellow seminary student sent me audio recordings and class notes from the lectures I was forced to miss after I was diagnosed. Second, several members of our congregation came over and cleaned our apartment one day, top to bottom, relieving Christy of the responsibility of having to do so herself. What stands out about those two examples is that, in both cases, those who cared for us did not wait for us to ask them for help. They came up with concrete proposals and then proactively sought us out to make them a reality. By their example those friends taught us a valuable lesson: though there are times when 'Let me know if there's anything I can do' is all that can be said, there are other times when a more proactive approach is called for. Instead of 'Let me know if there's anything I can do', try 'Let me tell you what I'd like to do to serve you.' Christy and I learned the value of others offering specific assistance without waiting for those in need to ask for it.

In short, the calling to 'allow others a place of service in our lives' never seemed so real to us as it did then. To be sure, there is a proper instinct that a person feels, to want to take responsibility for his own needs. Paul even urges the Thessalonians to work hard 'so that you may walk properly before outsiders and be dependent on no one' (*1 Thess.* 4:12). But there are times when that instinct must yield to the reality that we need others to step in and do things for us that, under normal circumstances, we would take care of ourselves. To live in practical denial of that reality, insisting in such moments that we are doing fine on our own, is to live in denial of the Lord himself. Consider: he is the one who brings us to a place of real neediness, and he is the one who surrounds us with those who are eager to step in.

And so Christy and I learned to let others serve us. In a host of ways. They sent class notes from seminary. They cleaned our apartment. They provided meals. They chauffeured me to medical appointments. They called and wrote and visited. They brought me European beer in the hospital. On and on this speech might go. But I think I hear the band.

FINDING COMPANY IN CHRIST

I write these things knowing full well that many who face trials do so without the rich blessings of family and church that we enjoyed. Some suffer almost entirely alone.

When that is the case, where do you begin?

You must begin here: do not suffer without the company of Christ.

Remember Samuel Rutherford, that seventeenth-century Scottish pastor? Here is what he wrote in another letter to that same woman we met in chapter 5, at a time when she was feeling isolated in the midst of trials:

> Worthy and dear lady, in the strength of Christ, fight and overcome. Ye are now yourself alone, but ye may have, for the seeking, three always in your company, the Father, Son, and Holy Spirit. I trust they are near you.[1]

[1] Rutherford, *Letters,* p. 52.

You see, the one whose faith is in Christ is never, finally, all alone. In Christ comes the divine promise, 'I will never leave you, nor forsake you' (*Heb.* 13:8). The Triune God of the Bible abides with the one who trusts in him. The believer always has the ministry of the Spirit, comforting and transforming, and he always has the truths and promises of the Word to cling to. Begin here. Walk with Christ. Talk to him in prayer. Learn from his Word. Count on his promises. Long for his heaven.

Then, trusting in Christ, make the most of the communion of the saints in Christ's church. If you have newly come to faith in Christ from outside the church, you must join a congregation of his people. Contrary to the spirit of our age, discipleship without membership (that is, church membership) is not a biblical option. And as a member of the body—whether new to Christ or a disciple of long-standing—learn to see your fellow church members as brothers and sisters in the Lord. View them as those to whom you are supernaturally bound by the Spirit (for that is what they are), and treat them like it with sacrificial love. Learn to see beyond earthly similarities and differences within the body and love others for Jesus' sake. Do not make the excuse, 'Well, your church sounds great, but I don't find mine to be all that loving.' You don't? Well, try this tune: 'Let there be practical love in the congregation to which I belong . . . and let it begin with me!' In other words, if you want to encourage tangible service among the members of your church, just do it.

For example, are you the one who is suffering alone, your trials and your needs unknown to others in the church? It may be that the first step is yours to take. You may have to go ahead and tell others about your needs before they inquire, and then ask them to help you in concrete ways before they offer. Remember: your duty—indeed, your privilege—is to let others serve you. Listen again to the Apostle Paul: 'Bear one another's burdens, and so fulfill the law of Christ' (*Gal.* 6:2). Would you deny your brothers and sisters in Christ the opportunity to fulfil his law? No, there is nothing heroic, nothing admirable, about shouldering your burdens, silent and solitary, if those burdens are plainly too heavy for you to bear alone.

Or, are you the one who has become aware of the needs of another? Then do not wait for him to ask for help. Step up and serve him. And if someone in your congregation is battling cancer, consider seeking and serving him months after he is diagnosed. By then he may have faded from people's minds. By then the flow of cards and visits and phone calls may have slowed considerably. That is a great time to show him what God is like, the God who promises never to leave, never to forsake.

In short, there is faithful giving, and there is faithful receiving, too. Model them both.

PREACHING AND HEARING

There is one more aspect of the church's life that we ought to consider in connection to suffering: the Lord uses faithful preaching to shape the hearts and minds of his people as they sit under that preaching Sunday after Sunday.

Christ, the Head of the church, has provided for our ongoing instruction in the truths of the gospel:

> And he gave the apostles, the prophets, the evangelists, the shepherds and teachers, to equip the saints for the work of ministry, for building up the body of Christ, until we all attain to the unity of the faith and of the knowledge of the Son of God, to mature manhood, to the measure of the stature of the fullness of Christ, so that we may no longer be children, tossed to and fro by the waves and carried about by every wind of doctrine, by human cunning, by craftiness in deceitful schemes (*Eph.* 4:11–14).

From the days of the apostles Christ has entrusted some with the official responsibility to proclaim God's Word to God's people. This is another way in which he has ensured that no Christian should have to go it alone. We need to be reminded regularly of God's grace and glory, and faithful pastors do just that as they preach from the pulpit and teach us in other settings. How valuable are those reminders in a world of suffering. In trying circumstances we need to cling to the goodness, wisdom and power of God, and ministers hold those very truths before our hearts when they declare the whole counsel of God.

This is yet another lesson I learned in my personal experience. I mean, my personal experience as a sermon hearer.

When I found out in April of 1999 that I had cancer, I had been a member of New Hope Presbyterian Church for over five years. If you count from the very first Sunday I visited, it was nearly six years. Week in and week out for those six years, the pastor of the congregation, Dave Coffin, steadily and faithfully proclaimed God's Word from the pulpit. Over and over again he taught us from the Scriptures concerning the comprehensive sovereignty and precious promises of God. In different ways and in different words he trained us concerning trials, reminding us that everything that comes to pass God brings to pass for his own glory and for the good of his people, encouraging us with the thought that no trial finally overthrows the gospel, for even death itself—the last trial—becomes the Christian's entrance into glory. Week after week he taught us.

And it was not just the sermons. It was also the congregational sermon discussions that he would lead after worship. It was also the after-dinner conversations in his living room in which I would pester him with too many questions about the Bible and theology, and he would patiently seek to answer each one. Plus the discussions over the phone. Plus the conversations in the car. Nearly six years of sermons and discussions, questions and answers, correction and encouragement. Week after week.

What neither of us realized was that during that whole time Dave was preparing me for the day when I would find out that I had cancer.

Of course, no one knew what my days would bring. No one knew in 1993 what I would learn on April 23, 1999. Dave did not know. I did not know. But looking back I can see now that the Lord was using Dave's steady, faithful, truth-full ministry all that time to fill my heart and mind with the very gospel realities that would hold me up when the MRI pictures went up on the screen.

There is an important lesson here for every Christian, since we are all sermon hearers. In short, we ought to see our relationship to preaching as a lifelong relationship. To be sure, it is good to consider each Sunday how the truth we have heard that day should shape our lives right away, but there is more to it than that. Each of us also ought to be storing up a deep reservoir of biblical convictions over the course of his life. Those convictions may pay off down the road in ways that you never anticipated.

Let us all be reminded of the good counsel that the *Westminster Larger Catechism* provides about hearing sermons:

Question 160: What is required of those that hear the word preached?

Answer: It is required of those that hear the word preached, that they attend upon it with diligence, preparation, and prayer; examine what they hear by the scriptures; receive the truth with faith, love, meekness, and readiness of mind, as the word of God; meditate, and confer of it; hide it in their hearts, and bring forth the fruit of it in their lives.

Notice that language, 'hide it in their hearts'. The Christian life is, among other things, from start to finish, a life of hearing sermons, and it is vital that we hold on to the truth we have heard. Who knows what the circumstances will be in which you will have to bring forth the fruit of the things you have stored away?

This is one of the reasons—and there are so many others—why the young people of the congregation, beginning at a reasonable age, ought to be present and attentive during the sermon. They ought to be there, listening and learning as best they can, even if the subject of the sermon might appear, at first glance, to have nothing to do with them at their age. First, that appearance is misleading. After all, there are principles in every faithful exposition of the Word that have to do with every disciple, young or old. Second, children ought to listen and learn because they are never too young to be storing up God's truth. No disciple is too young to start hiding the truth in his heart. Maybe when he is twenty-eight—or younger—he will find out that he has cancer. That is not the time to start thinking about the goodness, wisdom and power of God. Far better for him to have those truths already deeply rooted in his soul, thanks to years of faithful preaching and listening.

Notice that there is an important lesson here for preachers, too. Do not get caught in the trap of thinking that your fruitfulness in ministry is limited to the impact your sermon has on the day you preach it. Of course, it is a wonderful thing when a sermon hits a person 'in the moment', clearly and powerfully shaping his thinking and thus changing his living from that moment on. Certainly there were Sundays when the Lord used Dave's preaching to get my attention like that.

Sometimes the Lord is pleased to grant that kind of power to the preacher's words. In fact, sometimes the preacher himself is hit like that by his own words! But the lesson is this: there is more to the fruitfulness of preaching than those occasional instances of immediate impact.

The notion that a sermon is only as effective as the impression it makes in the moment can lead a man to try to preach sermons that are too clever, too tricky, too impressive. He succumbs to the temptation to try—and he tries this, wearily, each and every week—to pull a rabbit out of the hat as he expounds the text of Scripture. And then, as if he had just performed on some sort of reality TV show ('American Preacher Idol', perhaps?), he waits for members of the congregation to approach him after the worship service and give him his marks. Praise thrills him, which leads him to conclude, 'I've been fruitful in ministry.' Criticism devastates him, which leads him to resolve, 'I've failed. I'll just have to work that much harder to be impressive next week.' Idol, indeed!

Ministers face such pressure today to make their sermons relevant. Of course, relevance is a fine thing. The truths of the Bible are meant to shape our lives, and any ministry that treats those truths as mere abstractions, never touching down and addressing us as those who live on earth, is no true biblical ministry at all. So, yes, let us be relevant. But the danger we face is a too-narrow understanding of what relevant preaching looks like. You see, it is most relevant for a preaching ministry, over the long haul, to pour a steady stream of biblical truth into people's hearts and minds. With the blessing of the Lord, such preaching prepares Christians for the future as well as arming them for the present. It is sometimes said that the minister must seek in his sermon to meet the people where they are. That is a noble aspiration, of course, but the minister's job is also to get the people ready for where they will be. No, he cannot know precisely where their roads will take them, but he does know that the truths of Scripture are crucial to prepare them for every circumstance. So let him serve up a steady diet of those truths. Just think of it: the faithful preacher helps to foster spiritual emergency preparedness! Years ago I learned that lesson as a cancer patient, and I pray that I will never forget it now that I have become a preacher.

My fellow ministers, have you forgotten this lesson? Does your vision for ministry extend no further than next Sunday morning? Is your sense of fruitfulness in ministry determined solely by the comments you get about your sermon right after the worship service? Has it become your aim, perhaps without even realizing it, to wow the people who hear you preach? If so, it is time to change your aim: instead of wowing them in the moment, aim to feed them for a lifetime. Yes, that is hard work, requiring humility and patience year after year, but the Chief Shepherd grants grace to his servants for just this purpose. Look to him. Remember, he is the one who has provided preaching so that we will all 'attain to the unity of the faith and of the knowledge of the Son of God, to mature manhood, to the measure of the stature of the fullness of Christ' (*Eph.* 4:13). Since he himself has ordained preaching to that end, you can count on him to sustain you as you seek to be faithful.

Christ has said to his people, 'You'll never walk alone', promising above all his own abiding presence, and he has placed pastors in the church both to proclaim and to exemplify that fidelity. May we who preach labour in a manner worthy of that high calling, and may all who hear believe the Saviour's word. And may we do so throughout all the days that the Lord has appointed for us. Week after week.

Part 3: Life

CHAPTER SEVEN

Act 3: Ever Since

When we left our story at the end of Act 2, I had just undergone what would turn out to be my very last anti-cancer treatment, although we did not know at the time it was the last. We were still feeling a fair amount of uncertainty at that point concerning additional treatments and possible recurrence.

Thankfully, none of those fears was realized.

THE THRILL OF VICTORY

Best of all, we beat the cancer. As I mentioned before, as early as September my tests indicated that I was likely cancer-free. Follow-up tests in January showed the same thing: no more cancer.

But we knew that 'no more cancer *now*' does not necessarily mean 'no more cancer *ever*'. There was still the possibility of recurrence. We also knew that when cancer comes back, it can come back in a less treatable form. That is why my oncologist wanted to leave no treatment stone unturned: if there were any additional steps that might be worthwhile in my case, he wanted to consider them. That meant sending us to outside experts to get their counsel.

If you want to get expert cancer advice, there are several places on the East Coast that you can go. One of them is the Memorial Sloan-Kettering Cancer Center in Manhattan, New York City, which is where we ended up going. A doctor there agreed to review my medical records and to discuss with us the prospect of additional treatments. In particular, we wanted to ask him about a procedure known as a bone marrow transplantation (BMT, if you prefer yet another acronym). This is a procedure in which they blast the body with 'extra strength' chemotherapy, in doses so strong that it destroys your bone marrow, which is then replaced with healthy bone marrow taken either from a donor or from your own body beforehand. The question was: would that procedure make sense in my case, in order to decrease the likelihood of recurrence?

We were not terribly excited about the prospect of a bone marrow transplantation. Not only would the treatment itself be more gruelling than anything we had undergone to date, but the recovery period would be lengthy, too: I would be out of commission for weeks, if not months.

At that point I was in my last semester in seminary, with a May graduation in sight, but if we took this step all would have to be put on hold. Still, we resolved that if this doctor at Sloan-Kettering advised us to go ahead with the procedure, we would be willing. With all of that in mind, we packed our bags and drove off to New York.

Our appointment was set for Monday, March 13. There were several preliminary steps when we arrived at the Center: registration, waiting, blood tests, waiting, preliminary interviews, more waiting. In the meantime, behind the scenes, our doctor was looking over my records—everything from MRI films to blood analyses to written reports.

After all of that time and anticipation, when he finally came to meet with us we liked what he had to say. We liked it very much. He did not advise us simply that it would be unnecessary for me to undergo that extra treatment, or excessive, or ill-advised. He used a much better word. He pronounced that it would be *ludicrous* for me to do so. Now that is what I call definitive counsel! In his judgment, based upon the facts of my case, there was simply no reason for me to go through that gruelling process. We practically danced out of that hospital.

'Ludicrous' became our new favourite word. 'Ludicrous' meant no more chemotherapy. 'Ludicrous' meant no more worries about finishing the semester and graduating. 'Ludicrous' meant time to get back to normal life. Granted, even after that consultation in March we faced lingering fears about my cancer recurring. But even acknowledging those concerns this was as close as we had ever felt to reaching the end of our journey with cancer, nearly eleven months after it began. Finally we had a new date to remember. March 13, 2000: a date which will live in . . . acclamation!

BACK TO NORMAL

I can also report that after all of those months of cane-walking and stumbling and exercising and wondering and praying, I finally got my legs back.

Slowly but surely, over the course of the late summer and fall of 1999, I began to notice improvement in my walking. I became less dependent upon the cane, more confident with my steps. By the first Sunday in December, I was able to give up the cane for good.

And then, on a Saturday later that same month, I played tennis again for the first time. December is not a month when many go outside to play tennis, but that Saturday was just warm enough, and I was certainly eager enough. My parents were visiting for the weekend, and so the four of us—Mom, Dad, Christy and I, the same four who had made our way to the MRI centre on that April Friday—now made our way to the local tennis courts so that Dad and I could play.

It was not U. S. Open quality tennis, to be sure. I was still moving like a bit of a Frankenstein. I was not running down any difficult shots. But it was, without question, the sweetest session I ever spent on the courts. Remember those dreams I kept having throughout the summer and fall, dreams in which I could run again? Quite literally, my dreams came true. (Except for the bit about my forehand.) We have a photo that was snapped that day of my father and me, side-by-side, smiling, tennis rackets in hand.

I got back to my other favourite activities, too. Back to the basketball court with some of the men of our congregation. And then back to the trail with my wife. In January Christy and I went hiking on some snow-covered trails near Charlottesville, Virginia. The scenery was beautiful for anyone to see—a winter wonderland—but for me it was all the more breathtaking. It was a marvel to me that I was there, hiking in the midst of it with my own two legs.

There were other gradual changes that took place. My weight returned to normal. My sense of taste did, too. Pizza tasted like pizza again.

And, to top it off, I got my hair back.

Strangely, when my hair came back it came back wavy. We had heard rumours that hair sometimes returns in an altered state. That came true in my case. (Some men look good with wavy hair. Then there are the rest of us.) I even found that my parting was now on the other side of my head. Lo and behold, I had turned into a mirror image of my former self. Except for those waves. But eventually my hair got straightened out (literally), and my parting returned to the right side (which was my right side). All was well.

Plus, I still have all those hats.

EVER SINCE

Where did our story go from there? A few more noteworthy dates serve as milestones.

May 27, 2000. That was the date when I graduated from seminary. It was difficult for us to believe that we had actually reached that milestone, given what the past year had been like.

September 24, 2000. That was the date when I was ordained as a minister and installed as New Hope's first associate pastor. This congregation that had loved Christy and me so abundantly—now I would be serving them as an under-shepherd over the flock. Pastoral service has meant making quite a few hospital visits over the years. I am sure that I feel more at home in hospitals—for better or for worse—because of what we went through.

May 10, 2004. That was the date when I underwent my last PET scan. I had been returning to take that test once a year, and this one, just like all the others, showed no signs of cancer. My oncologist advised at that point that there was no need to keep going with them. No more scans.

Today I go back to see my oncologist for appointments twice a year. We have gotten to the point that we do not have to spend too much time talking about my condition, because there is practically no condition left for us to talk about. Still, it is good to go back on occasion and give a blood sample for testing, just in case.

Whenever I go in for those appointments, I find myself sitting in the waiting room side-by-side with those who still have a great deal to talk about with the oncologist, those who are still in the midst of the storm. There are patients, weakened, leaning on canes. There are friends and family members sitting alongside them, weakened and leaning in their own ways, in ways unseen. I find myself in the midst of a world that once was mine, but feeling like I do not quite belong there any more. I feel that strange tension of life in the midst of death. The Lord was pleased to preserve my life.

December 5, 2004. That was the date when Henry Fisher Wolfe and Philip Campbell Wolfe were born. June 27, 2006. That was the date when Charlotte Lillian Wolfe was born. Some things that happen in hospitals are good.

Of course, the birth of any child is a wondrous thing. But for

Christy and me the birth of our children was all the more marvellous. You see, almost from the day that I was diagnosed with cancer, our doctors prepared us for the possibility that my chemotherapy would wipe out not only my cancer but also my capacity to be a father. Chemotherapy does kill cancer cells, but it kills other cells, too, like reproductive cells. But in time God was pleased to give that back, too. And now he has given us these three. Now there are five disciples in the Wolfe family. We are still waiting to see if any of our children has perfect pitch.

MEMENTOS

Today, there are markers and mementos all around me that remind me of what we went through in 1999 and 2000.

Some of them are physical. I still have scars. I bear on my body the marks of cancer. No, nothing so visible as to frighten little children any more, but I know they are there.

I still have that cane, too. Lately I have placed it so that it rests over the door frame in my study. I do not pay much attention to it. For the most part it is out of sight up there. But every once in a while I do catch a glimpse of it, and then I am reminded of where I was and of what the Lord was pleased to give back.

These days, my children have taken an interest in that cane. For them it is a toy. They regularly ask me to get it down so that they can play with it. As you might imagine, that is quite a sight for this father to see. If the cane by itself reminds me of what the Lord was pleased to restore, then seeing it in the hands of my children does so all the more powerfully. That sight captures it all: life preserved, life restored, new life granted.

In part they are interested in my cane because they have seen the photo on a shelf nearby in which that cane is in my right hand, holding me up. It is a photo that was taken in August of 1999. One of my boys, when he first saw that photo, asked if it was a picture of

Grandpa! Now they know it is a picture of Daddy, taken at a time when Daddy was sick, many years ago.

The wonderful thing about that photo is that it stands right next to a second photo in the same frame. On the left is that picture of me in August of 1999, cane in hand. On the right is a very different picture: a photo of Christy, Henry, Philip and me taken on April 3, 2005, the day when the boys were baptized. That frame, with those two photos, was a gift from Christy on my first Father's Day. She had it inscribed: *'Soli Deo Gloria!'* To God alone be the glory.

Some of the mementos of my cancer experience exist in paper form. In a dusty box on a shelf in the garage I found a gold mine of cancer-related keepsakes stuffed between a bunch of old files.

First, that box contained copies of all my old medical reports. I am not a doctor, nor do I play one on TV, but there is plenty in those reports that is clear enough for even me to understand.

April 23, 1999, radiologist's report: 'This is a malignancy.'

April 28, 1999, pathology report: 'These findings are most consistent with a non-Hodgkin's lymphoma.'

September 29, 1999, PET scan report: 'No abnormal uptake is seen within the thoracic spine or the whole body that would suggest lymphoma.'

October 1, 1999, oncologist's report: 'The patient is now referred for radiation.'

And on and on the story goes, told in medical terms.

Second, that box held copies of all the emails that Christy and I sent to family and friends to keep them posted during our ordeal. They mark the milestones of our journey in a way that medical reports do not.

July 14, 1999: 'As far as Paul regaining neurological function, we continue to wait and pray.'

July 23, 1999: 'As soon as the pneumonia is licked, they can get back to the chemotherapy-then-radiation regimen that has been somewhat interrupted by all of this.'

August 12, 1999: 'Whether or not Paul will be able to return to his studies at Westminster Seminary in the fall remains a pretty big question mark.'

August 30, 1999: 'Last Friday, the 27th, we had our sixth and final round of chemotherapy . . . so all those nasty chemicals are now a thing of the past. Hooray! Now we get to see what kind of hair I'll have when it begins fully to grow back—we're told that it might be somewhat different than it was before, so we wait with some trepidation. Red and curly, perhaps?'

December 9, 1999: 'Also, this week I've begun to try "life without the cane." I'm still a little wobbly, but I'm hoping that we can make the cane an attic piece from now on.'

March 1, 2000: 'One small piece of news: we've finally been able to arrange for our consultation with a cancer specialist in New York City (at the Sloan Kettering Cancer Center) . . .'

March 14, 2000: 'We have just arrived back from our aforementioned trip to New York City, and there is news.'

Third, that box in the garage contained all the encouraging notes and get well cards that we received. We held on to those, and I am glad we did.

Even after all these years of being stuffed in a box in the garage, those notes and cards still give off the sweet aroma of Christian compassion and gospel certainty.

April 27, 1999: 'Dear Paul, Surely your Saviour is leading you and Christy through the deepest waters, and is asking you both to trust him with your lives. What else can you do, dear friend? This dark providence has consternated us all, and we cry out for you both. But it is only our dear Elder Brother who understands your sufferings, and through them is changing you from one degree of glory to another. We ever look to his mercy.'

May 1, 1999: 'Dear Paul, I found out this week that your sore back is whole lot more than your back. We will continue to pray for you and Christy during this time of trying from the hand of your heavenly Father. We can be sure that this present suffering is not worth comparing to the eternal weight of glory that is in store for us, and we can be sure that nothing will separate us from the love and power and fellowship of Christ Jesus our Lord.'

May 3, 1999: 'Dear Paul and Christy, We were startled to hear of Paul's surgery and diagnosis. More and more I know that "we know not what the future holds, only Him who holds it." We know He holds you both.'

In those excerpts, can you hear my friends teaching me the very lessons I am so eager to share with others now?

Finally, that box in the garage held a copy of the journal that I sat down and typed out beginning in April of 2000, around one year after my diagnosis day.

Yes, that means that I began to write my journal at a time when, for the most part, our battle with cancer was over. Why did I not keep a journal during our battle? I wanted to. I really did. I had a sense as we were going through it that I ought to be writing things down, recording thoughts, marking memories. But eventually I gave up the idea. I was just too exhausted, mentally and emotionally, to try take on a project like that. Some patients do have the strength to keep a journal. I was not one of them. Instead of being a blessing, I would have found the task to be an additional burden.

But in April of 2000, when the dust had settled, when I was not so tired any more, and while those thoughts and memories were still fresh in my mind, I finally sat down at the computer and began to record. Those fifty-one, single-spaced pages have proven invaluable to me, reminding me to this day of the events and emotions of our experience.

What strikes me now is how those four different collections of documents tell the same story from four different vantage points. My medical reports tell the story from the view of doctors and nurses acting in their professional capacities. The emails we sent recount it from the vantage point of the patient and his wife. The get-well cards we received tell the story from the perspective of those who loved us and suffered alongside us. And the journal I wrote records the story from the view of one who was looking back—with wonder—at what he had just gone through. All those papers piece together the memory of our experience, which is the memory of medicines and fears and love and gratitude.

There is one more memento that I found in that box in the garage: my temporary handicapped parking permit. Virginia Disabled Parking Placard Number 1294380. Expires July, 2004. It would have lasted me five years.

CHAPTER EIGHT

Confronting the Curse

On October 27, 2004, the Boston Red Sox reversed the Curse of the Bambino.

Legend has it that the Red Sox failed to win a World Series title after 1918 thanks to a curse that hovered over the team and its long-suffering fans. The Red Sox' owner, Harry Frazee, sold Babe Ruth ('the Bambino') to the New York Yankees in 1920, and the Boston franchise lived on a steady diet of postseason heartbreak thereafter . . . until they completed a four-game sweep of the St Louis Cardinals to win the 2004 World Series. Long-suffering, indeed: the Curse of the Bambino had outlasted the Soviet Union by more than ten years!

Remarkably the very next year the Chicago White Sox reversed a curse of their own, one that had lasted even longer. The story goes that the White Sox' failure to win a World Series championship after 1917 was attributable to a black cloud of scandal that had never blown away: eight White Sox were suspended from the team late in the 1920 season for having lost the Series deliberately the year before. The cloud only lifted, so the story goes, when the White Sox defeated the Houston Astros in 2005 for their first World Series trophy in eighty-eight years.

At present (here in 2009) Chicago Cubs fans keep waiting. The Cubs have not won the World Series since 1908. They have not even played in the World Series since 1945. Why not? Because of the Curse of the Billy Goat, of course! In 1945 a man and his goat were kicked out of a World Series game at Chicago's Wrigley Field. His anger led him (so they say) to place a curse on the team, and his curse has left the Cubs as non-champions ever since.

What do sports fans have in mind when they lament the curses or 'jinxes' that have kept their teams from glory? (Most are joking; some are not!) In short, they charge that some sinister unseen power—whether personal or impersonal—opposes their team, frustrating its best efforts, denying it ultimate victory. As a result, players and fans must somehow find a way to break the spell. Perhaps there is some 'Being' that must be appeased, or some incantation that must be recited, or some rite that must be performed . . . or some spectacular off-season trade that must be negotiated. Otherwise the heartbreak goes on.

Funny, right? Yes, when it comes to sports. But it would be careless to dismiss the category of 'curse' altogether, as if it were nothing more than the stuff of not-so-serious speculation about failures on the playing field. After all, life is frustrating—at times, even heartbreaking. There are anxieties in life that weigh far more heavily on our hearts than does the failure of our favourite team. Life is like that. Not only so, but in honest moments we admit that we are powerless to make it otherwise. Yes, 'one man can make a difference'—but even the most wonderful and lasting differences that man can introduce fail to alter the human condition in any fundamental sense. There are no incantations, no rites, no negotiations, by which we can make earthly life truly heavenly. There is no wind we can summon to disperse the clouds that hang over the human race.

Thankfully the Bible addresses these realities. In Scripture we find the diagnosis: yes, human experience is cursed. That is, life on earth is now characterized by difficulty and disappointment, and this is attributable not to the inscrutable opposition of some sinister unnamed power but to the just sentence of a holy God upon a sinful race. To make matters worse, our earthly difficulties remind us that there is a far more serious difficulty that confronts us—one that must be resolved before ultimate victory can be enjoyed—and it is the crisis that concerns the guilt of our sin against God. This is all very bad news. But to make matters far better, in Scripture we also find the cure: God has acted in grace and power in such a way as to deliver his people from this world of woe. In Jesus Christ, God has stepped in to reverse the curse, and to reverse it fully. This is very good news. This is the gospel.

THIS CLOUDY DAY

Let us consider the Scriptures' teaching.

There was nothing frustrating and heartbreaking about the creation in its original condition. Remember that God viewed it all as 'very good' when it was completed (*Gen.* 1:31). But sin changed everything. In Genesis 3 we read of the first rebellion of the first humans against God's good rule, and of the aftermath of that rebellion. Had they continued in obedience to God, no doubt their blessedness would have continued as well: delighting in God and in one another, cultivating together the marvellous creation he had entrusted to them, finding the created order to be a hospitable place for their life and service. Instead, in the wake of their sin, misery would mark their lives. In Genesis 3:14–19 God addresses himself directly to the various parties in the first human sin (Satan the instigator, and then Eve and Adam the sinners), and he solemnly pronounces that human life will now be characterized by pain, frustration and death.

The rest of the Bible fills out the picture, both in stories and in sermons. Famines force men to journey from place to place with their families in search of food (see Genesis 10, 26, 41–47). A whole society spirals downward into chaos and corruption, and this is the society of those who are expected to be devoted to God (see Judges). A woman who is pious and prayerful is unable to have children, and on top of that she must also bear the cruelty of another woman who has children and who torments her (see *1 Sam.* 1). A tower falls in Jerusalem and kills eighteen, and no easy explanation is at hand for why they were killed and not others (see *Luke* 13). Examples like these abound. Now our own experience in this world confirms the biblical testimony. Broken relationships. Broken bodies. Broken hearts. Broken lives. Life on earth is now lived under a cloud, and death, the last enemy, is always waiting, always mocking.

Because these are uncomfortable truths to contemplate, we are prone to push them out of our minds. As John Calvin observed, we are inevitably reminded of death from time to time (perhaps we hear of the death of another person, or even attend a funeral), but the impressions made upon our minds can be fleeting:

> If some corpse is being buried, or we walk among graves, because the likeness of death then meets our eyes, we, I confess, philosophize brilliantly concerning the vanity of this life. Yet even this we do not do consistently, for often all these things affect us not one bit. But when it happens, our philosophy is for the moment; it vanishes as soon as we turn our backs, and leaves not a trace of remembrance behind it. In the end, like applause in the theatre for some pleasing spectacle, it evaporates.[1]

Though our sense of our mortality may evaporate, the reality of it does not. After all, truths pushed out of our minds do not thereby cease to be true. Unyielding, death remains the culmination of the sorrows of life.

Of course, these earthly consequences pale next to the ultimate consequence of human sin: man now finds himself alienated from

---

[1] John Calvin, *Institutes of the Christian Religion*, ed. John T. McNeill, tr. Ford Lewis Battles, vol. 1 (Philadelphia: Westminster Press, 1960), p. 714.

God. As Paul reminds the Ephesians, we 'were by nature children of wrath, like the rest of mankind' (*Eph.* 2:3), and he includes himself, the once-devoted Jew, in that estimation. The Bible's double-use of the word 'death' is telling: there is *physical* death—the disintegration of the human person, the separation of body and soul—and there is *spiritual* death—the fracturing of Creator-creature fellowship because man is sinful and God is holy. (For these two uses of 'death', see *John* 11:25–26 and *Rev.* 2:10–11.) When a man considers the certainty of his own physical death and sees others meet that fate before him, he is rightly pierced with the thought of what physical death signifies: the revelation of the wrath of God against human sin and the prospect of the eternal experience of that wrath. In sum, the brokenness of life on earth reminds him that man is broken off from heaven, and that no one on earth has the power to repair the breach. The fears, frustrations and failings of this life are tokens of something far more fearful.

Such is the state of affairs for man apart from the gospel of Jesus Christ. Mercifully there is a gospel of Jesus Christ, yet for believers and unbelievers alike the earthly dimension of the misery inaugurated in Genesis 3 remains a fact of life. Paradoxically, the Bible's teaching concerning the Fall and its fallout helps us to make sense of the sorrowful condition in which we find the world today . . . including many circumstances that do not appear to make sense at all. One student prepares diligently for his exam and fails; the lazy student next to him guesses on every question and passes. Where is the sense in that? A beloved husband and father is killed in his thirties by a drunk driver; a clever criminal lives to see ninety. Who can explain it? 'In my vain life I have seen everything. There is a righteous man who perishes in his righteousness, and there is a wicked man who prolongs his life in his evildoing' (*Eccles.* 7:15). Cells in one man's body go haywire for no apparent reason; another man who lives and eats and exercises just like the first man gets a clean bill of health. What made him to differ? A terrorist detonates a bomb in a restaurant and in an instant scores are killed, some who were good in terms of civic virtue and some who were not, and the terrorist's blood mixes with theirs. On the surface there seems to be no sense, no order in such developments.

But viewed in the light of the Bible's teaching concerning sin and curse, there is a kind of sense in them after all. It makes perfect sense that life should be like this, given the fact that the human race continues in rebellion against our holy Creator. A world full of frustrations and failings, chaos and corruption, illness and injustice: given the Fall, what else would we expect? We may not be able to explain why one person gets cancer and his neighbour does not, but we can hardly wonder that there is cancer in the world to begin with. It is not uncommon in Christian literature to find the human condition described in terms of 'sin and misery,' and that pairing is most biblical. Given sin and God's just sentence against it, should we be surprised by misery, even misery that confounds us?

It is not that life is utterly devoid of blessing. Not at all. Life itself is a blessing, and God is pleased to protect and provide for his creatures in a variety of ways. The Psalmist prays, 'You cause the grass to grow for the livestock and plants for man to cultivate, that he may bring forth food from the earth and wine to gladden the heart of man, oil to make his face shine and bread to strengthen man's heart' (*Psa.* 104:14–15). But we must acknowledge that difficulty and disappointment still permeate our experience, even some of its sweetest moments. It is not dour to say so, only honest.

A moment in the 1987 film *Good Morning, Vietnam* hauntingly captures this reality. Robin Williams' character, the radio disc jockey Adrian Cronauer, plays for his soldier-listeners a recording of Louis Armstrong singing 'What a Wonderful World'. Armstrong sings of green trees and red roses, blue skies and white clouds, blessed days and sacred nights, handshakes and warm greetings and love among friends. As the song plays, a Vietnam video montage plays with it. Though at first several of the images seem serene, the footage soon turns dreadful. Scenes of bombings and killings. Visions of sadness and fear. An uprising is violently put down. Young men wield the weapons of war. Finally the song concludes with the refrain: 'And I think to myself, what a wonderful world.' The contrast between song and scenes is jarring. Yes, there is beauty and blessedness and love in the world—the song is right about that—but there is also death and sadness and warfare—the video is right, too.

In the face of such realities, we can only cry out, 'Who will deliver us from this world of death?' More to the point, 'Who will lead us to a world of life?'

THE MISSION OF THE MESSIAH

God himself set the stage in the Old Testament for the great work of redemption that he had planned. With prophetic promises he stirred earnest expectations in the hearts of his people that one day he would reverse the curse, relieving them of the sin and misery in which the human race had been mired since the Fall.

In Isaiah 65:17–25 the prophet painted a picture of the new world the Lord intended to create: a world of joy and gladness, security and satisfaction, life and love and harmony among creatures. Most importantly, he described a world of harmony with God: 'Before they call I will answer; while they are yet speaking I will hear' (*Isa.* 65:24). Elsewhere Isaiah made it clear that death itself will have been defeated, along with the mourning that goes with it: 'He will swallow up death forever; and the Lord GOD will wipe away tears from all faces, and the reproach of his people he will take away from all the earth, for the LORD has spoken' (*Isa.* 25:8).

Those were grand promises, indeed. The thoughtful Israelite must have had some sense that grand and unprecedented things would have to happen in order for those promises to be kept. With the benefit of hindsight, we know what those lofty salvation requirements were. A Saviour would have to come who was qualified both to deal with death and to create life, one who could resolve the dilemma of our Fall as well as remain standing in perfect righteousness himself. No mere man would do.

We know that those were the requirements because we have the advantage of knowing the one who gloriously satisfied them all! Jesus Christ—no mere man, but a God-man—came uniquely qualified to deliver us from this world of death and to lead us into that new world of life.

The writer of Hebrews teaches us that Jesus Christ is God in the flesh: 'He is the radiance of the glory of God and the exact imprint of his nature, and he upholds the universe by the word of his power' (*Heb.* 1:3). The author goes on throughout that opening chapter to reinforce the claim that Jesus is divine. And yet this same writer teaches us that this same Jesus is human, made like us in every respect except that he was without sin (2:14–18, 4:15). His was a true human nature, a genuine human life, real human sufferings. He came and willingly walked with us through this vale of tears though he himself deserved no sorrow. Throughout his life he was surrounded by sin and buffeted by misery. To be sure, his was no joyless life; the Gospel records make that clear. Yet in his experience of the post-Fall human condition another of Isaiah's prophecies came true: 'He was despised and rejected by men; a man of sorrows, and acquainted with grief' (*Isa.* 53:3).

The good news is that he came and lived with us under the cloud not merely to keep us company but to deliver us from that cloud altogether. Solidarity with our Saviour is the truth (*Heb.* 4:15), but it is not the whole truth. He had come not merely to comfort us in our misery *here*, but finally to lead us into an eternal *There*, where sorrows will be no more. Throughout his earthly ministry Jesus gave glimpses of that new world in his words and deeds. Many of the miracles he performed served as signs of his curse-reversing mission, signalling that the kingdom he had come to inaugurate would be a very different world indeed:

> instead of oppression, liberty (*Luke* 4:31–37)
> instead of sickness, health (4:38–39)
> instead of frustration, success (5:1–11)
> instead of ostracism, fellowship (5:12–14)
> instead of disability, power (5:17–26)
> instead of death, life (7:11–17)
> instead of chaos, calm (8:22–25)
> instead of emptiness, abundance (9:10–17)

But Jesus knew that the creation of that kingdom would not come without cost. Remember, cursedness had come to cloud creation because of man's alienation from God. The miseries of this life were always tokens of the greatest misery of all, which is that man in his sin is the well-deserved object of the wrath of God. Thus, earthly life, now broken, could only be mended if divine wrath were first taken away. And divine wrath could only be taken away if a divine person stepped forward to receive it in our place.

And he did.

'Christ redeemed us from the curse of the law by becoming a curse for us—for it is written, "Cursed is everyone who is hanged on a tree"' (*Gal.* 3:13). The real dilemma that had to be resolved was the dilemma of our guilt before our holy Creator, and Christ took care of that on the cross. There he placed our guilt upon his own shoulders and bore the divine anger that we deserved.

As Paul puts it in 2 Corinthians 5, 'For our sake he [God] made him [Christ] to be sin who knew no sin, so that in him we might become the righteousness of God' (*2 Cor.* 5:21). Here is the great exchange of the gospel. Christ took the guilt of our sin and suffered what we justly deserved, and now he gives us the status of his righteousness and the heavenly inheritance that he justly gained. Back in the Garden God summoned our first parents to walk in righteousness before him . . . and they failed. The result was all of the cursedness—both natural and supernatural—that we have been considering. But Jesus Christ stepped in to save, living and dying and rising. And because he did so his people have been reconciled to God and now look forward with longing to God's new world. In Romans 8 Paul sheds glorious light on just how new that new world will be:

> For the creation waits with eager longing for the revealing of the sons of God. For the creation was subjected to futility, not willingly, but because of him who subjected it, in hope that the creation itself will be set free from its bondage to corruption and obtain the freedom of the glory of the children of God. For we know that the whole creation has been groaning together in the pains of childbirth until now. And not only the creation, but we ourselves, who have the firstfruits of the Spirit, groan inwardly as we wait eagerly for adoption as sons, the redemption of our bodies (*Rom.* 8:19–23).

According to Paul, the created order around us will one day enjoy liberation from its present condition. Plus, believers will receive the redemption of their bodies. Those who trust in Christ have already become the children of God (*1 John* 3:1), but in this life they have bodies that do not fit that glorious identity. Their present bodies, like those of everyone else, are wasting away (*2 Cor.* 4:16), perishable, dishonourable and weak (*1 Cor.* 15:42-43). Imagine the children of God, clothed like that! Consider the children of the King, draped in torn and tattered rags! But Paul assures us that one day God's children by adoption will receive bodies that match their identity (verse 23 above, 'adoption as sons, the redemption of

our bodies'), bodies that will be imperishable, glorious and powerful (*1 Cor.* 15:42–43). At last the sons and daughters of God will
be properly attired: heavenly bodies for the children of heaven who
are living and serving there.

When will these things be? On the Day when Christ returns to
earth to usher in eternity. As Paul writes to the Philippians: 'But
our citizenship is in heaven, and from it we await a Saviour, the
Lord Jesus Christ, who will transform our lowly body to be like
his glorious body, by the power that enables him even to subject all
things to himself' (*Phil.* 3:20–21). Until that day, those in heaven
with Jesus live as souls without bodies, but on that day, all will be
clothed, all will be glorified.

What a wonderful gospel God has revealed for our salvation!
It is true to say that Jesus comforts the believer in this life (*John*
14:27). It is also true to say that the believer will go to be with Jesus
at death (*Phil.* 1:23). But the gospel is much more: salvation entails nothing less than resurrection. New world. New bodies. New
creation. Our experience of salvation follows a 'good/better/best'
pattern:

> it is very *good* to know God through Christ in this life;
> it is even *better* to enter into the presence of Christ at death;
> it will be *best* of all when Christ returns to earth at the end of
> time.

Only then will he bring all things to completion. Only then
will the original creation design have come to fruition: man, made
body-and-soul, made for life in society lived in love for God, will
have been finally, thoroughly raised.

> And I heard a loud voice from the throne saying, 'Behold, the
> dwelling place of God is with man. He will dwell with them,
> and they will be his people, and God himself will be with them
> as their God. He will wipe away every tear from their eyes, and

death shall be no more, neither shall there be mourning, nor crying, nor pain any more, for the former things have passed away'
(*Rev.* 21:3–4).

DEATH AND THE CHRISTIAN

Of course, that glorious final day has not yet arrived. That is why (as Paul puts it in Romans 8) we are still longing, still groaning for that which is yet to be. Christ has not yet returned to usher in the age to come. This age, death included, rages on. Believers are not exempted from death. The *Westminster Larger Catechism* helps us to understand this:

Question 85: Death, being the wages of sin, why are not the righteous delivered from death, seeing all their sins are forgiven in Christ?

Answer: The righteous shall be delivered from death itself at the last day and even in death are delivered from the sting and curse of it; so that, although they die, yet it is out of God's love, to free them perfectly from sin and misery, and to make them capable of further communion with Christ, in glory, which they then enter upon.

Yes, those who trust in Christ still die (and they experience the sorrows of this life along the way), but for them the sting of death has been removed. For them death no longer means what it used to mean. It no longer has the power to terrify them, reminding them of the wrath to come, because thanks to Christ they have been delivered from that wrath: 'For God has not destined us for wrath, but to obtain salvation through our Lord Jesus Christ' (*1 Thess.* 5:9). No wonder that Paul, having reflected at length on the resurrection in 1 Corinthians 15, finally exclaims, '"O death, where is your victory? O death, where is your sting?" The sting of death is sin, and the power of sin is the law. But thanks be to God, who gives us the victory through our Lord Jesus Christ' (*1 Cor.* 15:55–57). This was Christ's saving aim from the outset: 'Since therefore the children share in flesh and blood, he himself likewise partook of the same things, that through death he might destroy the one who has the power of death, that is, the devil, and deliver all those who through fear of death were subject to lifelong slavery' (*Heb.* 2:14-15). The devil, that great accuser, has been spectacularly disarmed when it comes to the Christian: he has nothing truly terrifying left to say; the Christian has nothing left to fear. 'There is therefore now no condemnation for those who are in Christ Jesus' (*Rom.* 8:1). This is why our *Catechism* can confess that death now comes to believers 'out of God's love'. Death is now God's means of liberating the believer and bringing him home.

We see this reflected in a remarkable letter that Martin Luther, the great pioneer Reformer of the sixteenth century, wrote to his father when he learned that his father was seriously ill. In that letter Luther the son became also Luther the pastor, encouraging his father that because of Christ the believer need not cower in fear of death:

> Therefore let your heart now be bold and confident in your illness, for we have there, in the life beyond, a true and faithful helper at God's side, Jesus Christ, who for us has strangled death, together with sin, and now sits [in heaven] for us; together with all the angels he is looking down on us, and awaiting us, so that when we are to depart, we dare not worry or fear that we might sink or fall to the ground. His power over death and sin is too great for them to harm us. . . . May he, our dear Lord and Saviour, be with you and at your side, so that (may God grant it to happen either here or there) we may joyfully see each other again. For our faith is certain, and we don't

doubt that we shall shortly see each other again in the presence of Christ.[2]

Listen to Luther: Jesus Christ has 'strangled' death on behalf of his people, so that 'we dare not worry or fear'. Learn from Luther: death has been conquered for the Christian. Luther wrote that letter on February 15, 1530. His father, Hans Luther, died less than four months later, on May 29. Martin himself followed on February 18, 1546. They have basked in the presence of Christ ever since.

This same truth is also reflected in Bunyan's *Pilgrim's Progress*. In the second part of that work, Bunyan imaginatively chronicles the journey of the woman Christiana on her way to the Celestial City. Near the end, he describes the moment when Christiana receives word that her time has come to leave this life behind, including dear family and friends:

> Now, while they lay here, and waited for the good hour, there was a noise in the town, that there was a post come from the Cœlestial City, with matter of great importance to one Christiana, the wife of Christian the Pilgrim. So enquiry was made for her, and the house was found out where she was, so the post presented her with a letter: The contents whereof were, Hail, good woman! I bring thee tidings, that the Master calleth for thee, and expecteth that thou shouldest stand in his Presence, in clothes of Immortality, within this ten days.
>
> When he had read this letter to her, he gave her therewith a true token that he was a true messenger, and was come to bid her make haste to be gone, The token was, an Arrow with a point sharpened with Love, let easily into her heart, which by degrees

---

[2] Martin Luther, 'To Hans Luther, Wittenberg, February 15, 1530,' in *Luther's Works*, vol. 49, Letters II, ed. and tr. Gottfried G. Krodel (Philadelphia: Fortress Press, 1972), pp. 269-71. In his introduction to this letter, Krodel gives it high praise: 'This letter is among the finest of Luther's writings' (p. 267).

wrought so effectually with her, that at the time appointed she must be gone.[3]

You see, when death came to Christiana, it came by 'an arrow sharpened with love'. Her Master was calling for her, intending that she should stand before him in immortality. Every Christian ought to contemplate his own death along those same lines. It is not that death is now pleasant. Let us not pretend that it is. But the wonder of the gospel is that grace has conquered and enlisted even the dreadful things of the curse to advance the Saviour's cause. Death is still rightly called 'the last enemy' (*1 Cor.* 15:26), but for the believer the last enemy has already been transformed thanks to the grace of our greatest Friend.

TRUTH APPLIED

What did all of this mean to Christy and me as we made our way down a dark road?

It meant several things.

First, it meant that there was a sense in which my getting cancer made perfect sense. No, we had no idea why I got cancer as opposed to others, or why my cells went bad in the way they did, but we were not thrown into a tailspin of confusion, wondering why terminal illness exists in the first place and charging God with wrongdoing as we did so. Come to grips with Genesis 3 (the account of the Fall) and you will enjoy a certain steadiness of heart and mind in the face of bad news. We were not perfectly steady, to be sure, but we were steadier than we would have been otherwise. What the Scriptures have to say concerning sin and curse are not the happiest of truths to consider, but like all Scripture teachings they are profitable (*2 Tim.* 3:16). They pay off. When you are diag-

---

[3] John Bunyan, *The Pilgrim's Progress* (Edinburgh: Banner of Truth, 1977), pp. 369–70.

nosed with cancer and then have to be treated for it, they pay off quite remarkably.

Second, these truths meant that we were freed up to cry out to God. We knew that human life is now lived under a curse and that my getting cancer was a part of that. There was no effort to pretend (with others, least of all with God) that things were not that bad, that this was little more than a minor setback, and that the administration of a few helpful drugs would quickly get us back to heaven . . . as if we had been living a life of heavenly bliss before we were so rudely interrupted. God's Word had injected too much realism into our spiritual bloodstream to think like that. I love to listen to our Tony Bennett recordings, but whenever I listen to him sing the song 'Smile', I thank God that this is not the gospel:

> Smile though your heart is aching.
> Smile even though it's breaking.
> When there are clouds in the sky, you'll get by.
> If you smile through your fear and sorrow
> Smile and maybe tomorrow
> You'll see the sun come shining through for you.
> Light up your face with gladness.
> Hide every trace of sadness
> Although a tear may be ever so near.
> That's the time you must keep on trying.
> Smile, what's the use of crying?
> You'll find that life is still worthwhile
> If you just smile.[4]

Lovely voice. Lovely arrangement. Lousy theology. No, when we were facing and fighting cancer, we followed the lead of our Elder Brother, who 'offered up prayers and supplications, with loud cries and tears' (*Heb.* 5:7). Jesus was realistic about life in this present

---

[4] Lyrics by John Turner and Geoffrey Parsons, 1954.

evil age, and he prayed accordingly. He wept accordingly. That man of sorrows did not sing 'Smile'. Rather, his were the laments of the Psalter. In this respect, too, we servants are not above our Master.

Third, and most precious, these truths meant that ours was an invincible hope. Cancer does have a kind of deathly power, but its power is pitiful weakness compared with the resurrection power of the gospel. As one whose faith was in the risen Christ, I knew that I could not lose! After all, the worst that cancer could do was to take my life . . . and had that happened I would have immediately entered into Life as I had never known it before.

Remember the counsel of the *Larger Catechism* that I cited before: had death come it would have come out of God's love, perfectly freeing me from sin and misery, making me capable of a communion with Christ that this world cannot afford. Not only so, but I also knew that God would certainly use my death (as he uses every circumstance, bright or bitter) in some way to advance his own good purposes in the lives of the still-living. Finally, I had the unshakeable hope of receiving a resurrection body in the end. Even if my present body were to break down in death, I still had a far more wonderful embodied life to look forward to. I must confess: my thinking and feeling were not all faithfulness. I knew (as many Christians know in such circumstances) an undercurrent of doubt and discouragement. But there was a measure of real hopefulness in my heart all the same, and it was there thanks to the one who had borne the wrath of God and removed the sting of death.

A remarkable moment in a seminary classroom drove this lesson home.

Actually, for me it was a remarkable moment in my living room in Virginia. Unable to travel to Pennsylvania for my seminary classes in the early days of my treatment, I kept up with my courses by listening to audio recordings of the lectures I missed. During one of those class sessions our professor was asked a sobering question related to the killings at Columbine High School in Littleton, Colorado, which had happened just days before. (The Columbine shootings took place on April 19; I was diagnosed on April 23; this question-and-answer session took place on April 27.) The question ran something like this: put yourself there in Littleton. What might you say to grieving families who are trying to make sense of such a dreadful event?

Our professor made several points in reply. One of those points arrested me then, and it sticks with me today. Speaking about those who face death with firm faith in Christ, he said this: 'We also have to learn that sometimes an individual's greatest contribution is the way he or she dies.'

As you might imagine, that remark got my attention as I sat there listening in my living room in Virginia, cancer and chemotherapy doing battle within my body in that very moment. Sometimes people die younger than we think is right. Sometimes people die suddenly, ripped without warning from their loved ones. Sometimes people die at the hands of human evil, as those students did. But in the gospel economy, death is trumped. The one who dies leaving behind a legacy of faithfulness to Christ has given a gift that far outweighs the circumstances of his death, however sudden, however tragic. What our professor had meant as a reply to a classroom question I received as a summons to Christian discipleship: live well (that is, live hopefully in Christ) and you will have taken a big step in the direction of dying well, for you will have helped others to look to Christ even after you are gone.

Fourth, these truths guarded us from confusing healing with resurrection. To be honest, I should say that these truths should have guarded me from that confusion. I admit, this was a lesson I had to learn, inclined as I was to make physical restoration (meaning, restoration to the tennis court) my highest aspiration.

God in his wisdom used a friend and fellow tennis player to teach me.

This friend and I were catching up over lunch at a time when I had regained most of my mobility. Naturally, I was thrilled to have my legs back and to be playing sports again. My dreams had come true!

He shared my joy, fellow tennis player that he was. But he also said something in the course of that conversation that was quite convicting. He observed, almost in passing, that in the grand scheme of things the regaining of my mobility amounted to a kind of delay, a temporary restoration, because in this present evil age the outer man (even that of the hale and hearty) is still wasting away. He did not put the point exactly in those terms, but that was the thrust.

Now, he did not say what he said to be cruel, aiming to pour cold water on my enthusiasm. As I mentioned, he did share my joy, and this other remark had the feel of a 'by the way'. And yet he said it in such a way as to bring me to my senses. He was right. Yes, my legs worked again, and that was a tremendous blessing from the Lord, a gift not to be despised. I was right to thank him for it. But the outer man—including my outer man—was still wasting away. That had not changed. Yes, the Lord had been pleased to improve my condition in this life, but that was the point: I was still here, in this life, not yet raised, still under the cloud, still facing death. Regaining life and mobility thanks to surgery and medicines and physical therapy was wonderful . . . but it did not amount to resurrection. I had become so obsessed with playing sports again that I had lost sight of the fleeting and fragile character of life in this world, even life at its strongest and fullest.

It was yet another reminder that the gospel ought to lift our gaze beyond the horizon of this life, with all of its heights and depths, to the eternal summit of resurrection glory. In this life the

Lord gives, and the Lord takes away. Whether he does the one or the other, you must 'set your hope fully on the grace that will be brought to you at the revelation of Jesus Christ' (*1 Pet.* 1:13).

THE CHRISTIAN PILGRIM

The importance of heavenly-mindedness was one of the lessons that Christy and I had to learn in the face of cancer, and it has been a lesson to hold on to ever since. As Paul urged the Colossians: 'If then you have been raised with Christ, seek the things that are above, where Christ is, seated at the right hand of God. Set your minds on things that are above, not on things that are on earth' (*Col.* 3:1–2). Notice that the believer rightly fixes his gaze on heaven even when things are going well for him here on earth. These truths are meant not merely to console us in times of sorrow, but also to stir us in times of abundance. The healthy man, as well as the cancer patient, ought to set his heart and mind on the new world.

I am more mindful now than I used to be of heaven as my destination, more self-conscious of my identity as a pilgrim. Cancer impressed those realities upon me. So did the death of a faithful seminary professor (Al Groves, the man who taught me from Isaiah that very semester when I was diagnosed), and then the death of my faithful mother-in-law just a few months later. (It was cancer in both cases.) So have opportunities to preach and teach about heaven over these years.

I have thought many times of the Charlie Peacock song in which he sings, 'I want to live like heaven is a real place.' Sadly, how often do I find myself living like it is fictional! This place that I have never seen, this world that I can barely imagine: it is as real as the Virginia home in which I live with my wife and children today. It is populated even now with countless souls and with Christ himself, all looking forward to the day of his return. Like Bunyan's Christian and Christiana, I live best when I live fixed on the Celestial City, pressing on.

Consider the counsel of Jonathan Edwards, the great eighteenth-century American theologian and preacher. In a sermon entitled 'The Christian Pilgrim', Edwards taught his hearers that 'this life ought to be so spent by us, as to be only a journey or pilgrimage towards heaven'.[5] In order to cultivate that pilgrim mindset among his listeners, Edwards drew upon observations from every-day experience:

> A traveller is not wont to rest in what he meets with, however comfortable and pleasing, on the road. If he passes through pleas-ant places, flowery meadows, or shady groves; he does not take up his content in these things, but only takes a transient view of them as he goes along. He is not enticed by fine appearances to put off the thought of proceeding. No, but his journey's end is in his mind. If he meets with comfortable accommodations at an inn, he entertains no thoughts of settling there. He considers that these things are not his own, that he is but a stranger, and when he has refreshed himself, or tarried for a night, he is for going forward. And it is pleasant to him to think that so much of the way is gone.[6]

Later in that same sermon, Edwards challenged his hearers to compare the blessedness of this life with that of the life to come:

> To go to heaven, fully to enjoy God, is infinitely better than the most pleasant accommodations here. Fathers and mothers, husbands, wives, or children, or the company of earthly friends, are but shadows; but the enjoyment of God is the substance.

[5] Jonathan Edwards, 'The Christian Pilgrim, or The True Christian's Life a Journey Towards Heaven', in *The Works of Jonathan Edwards*, vol. 2 (Edinburgh: Banner of Truth, 1995), p. 243.
[6] Edwards, *Works*, vol. 2, p. 243.

These are but scattered beams; but God is the sun. These are but streams; but God is the fountain. These are but drops; but God is the ocean.[7]

In short, the believer is on his way to God. Relying upon grace he presses on, not allowing any earthly possessions or circumstances to distract him from his pilgrim-mission. He views all things in the light of the glory of God, and he does so as one who has God as his chief portion and delight. Here is a man who simply will not be denied. He will reach the City. He will reach the very presence of God.

A PIERCING QUESTION

When Jesus went to Bethany four days after the death of his friend Lazarus, Lazarus's sister Martha came out to meet him. Even at that point prior to his death and resurrection, Martha had some sense that Jesus possessed death-denying power: 'Martha said to Jesus, "Lord, if you had been here, my brother would not have died"' (*John* 11:21). Their remarkable and poignant conversation goes on, and the subject is resurrection. Finally, Jesus makes yet another of his staggering 'I am' claims: 'Jesus said to her, "I am the resurrection and the life. Whoever believes in me, though he die, yet shall he live, and everyone who lives and believes in me shall never die. Do you believe this?"' (verses 25–26).

What a moment! What a question! As we have considered before, it is one thing to be told that the gospel is true; it is another thing to be interrogated as to whether or not we believe that it is true. And it is another thing altogether (and here we find Martha) to be interrogated face-to-face by the God-man who is the gospel. Martha responds, professing her faith: 'She said to him, "Yes, Lord; I believe that you are the Christ, the Son of God, who is coming into the world"' (verse 27).

[7] Edwards, *Works*, vol. 2, p. 244.

As I have pondered Jesus' piercing question in recent years—'Do you believe this?'—it has struck me that that question confronts us at every turn. The Bible teaches us many things, and over and over again, in moments of joy and sorrow in our lives, Jesus asks us through his Word, 'Do you believe this?' Imagine that question as a watermark printed on every page of your Bible, faintly visible behind every truth you find there, always challenging, always confronting. The question is not simply, 'Do you agree that this is true?', but more fully, 'Will you now live (thinking, feeling, speaking, acting, striving, rejoicing) as one who agrees that this is true?'

We have reflected upon several of those biblical truths here in this chapter. A cloud of cursedness now rests over the creation. The wrath of God is revealed against this sinful human race. We are powerless on our own to undo the deathly damage that we have done. Christ came in power to accomplish what we could not, destroying death and gaining life by his own life and death on our behalf. Because he did so, a whole new world awaits us, a resurrection world. Because he did so, even death has been disarmed. Jesus is the Resurrection and the Life. And he asks you,

'Do you believe this?'

CHAPTER NINE

'And So to Him I Leave It All'

Over nine years have passed since our cancer odyssey came to a close. Strange though it may seem, I have found that surviving cancer presents its own problems. You might think that for the survivor the problems are all past. Think again! I have discovered three challenges that face the one who has passed through trial seemingly unscathed. I name them Presumption, Paralysis and Pouting.

To name them like that makes them sound like sinister characters that Bunyan's Christian might have encountered as he made his progress as a pilgrim. Come to think of it, perhaps that is precisely how we should conceive of them. These are three fiends.

PRESUMPTION

The first of these challenges is the temptation to start boasting about tomorrow all over again. If you are not careful you can find yourself thinking like this:

Oh, I get it. I *am* living my own script after all. My cancer, well, that was just a temporary glitch in the narrative. Now we're back on track. Now I can see how it's all going to turn out, and how we're going to get there. Kids with perfect pitch, here they come! Golden years with an adequate retirement account, we're on our way! In fact, now my script is even better! For the rest of my life I can rest easy, because now my PSQ (Personalized Suffering Quota) has been filled! I may not reach the age of 175 like Abraham, but it must be that I'm destined to die like Abraham 'in a good old age, an old man and full of years'!

Oops. Notice all of those exclamation marks?

Do you see what I have done? I have muddled my spiritual punctuation again. Exclamation marks where question marks belong. I have slipped back into the same old errors. Boasting about tomorrow. Claiming to know what my days will bring. Putting promises into God's mouth. The only difference is that now I am doing all of that after cancer, as opposed to before my diagnosis or during my treatment. In fact, the one who has endured some crisis may even feel that he is entitled to such certainty. 'After all,' he reasons, 'I've paid my dues. God owes me. God owes me the same sort of "happily ever after" that he once gave to Job.'

PARALYSIS

The second post-cancer temptation takes us to the opposite extreme, which is to succumb to paralyzing fear. Some who have passed through cancer and who have been given a clean bill of health on the other side find themselves haunted by the prospect that their cancer will come back, or that some other threat will arise, or that some other great calamity will befall them.

Imagine the one in whose life this fear is especially palpable. Prior to his illness he may have enjoyed a certain blissful ignorance, relatively unaware of serious dangers and deep sorrows. But then cancer changed everything. Now his eyes have been opened to those dangers and sorrows in a personal way. Now he lives obsessed with the prospect of What Might Happen Next. Forgetting Jesus' counsel ('Therefore do not be anxious about tomorrow, for tomorrow will be anxious for itself. Sufficient for the day is its own trouble'—*Matt.* 6:34), he piles a lifetime's worth of worry on to his shoulders today, and of course that burden is enormous. His fear so weighs him down that he finds it nearly impossible to stand up and live. 'Anxiety in a man's heart weighs him down' (*Prov.* 12:25). Just getting out of bed in the morning is a Herculean task. He has become skittish about routine medical appointments (there may be another devastating diagnosis), reluctant to travel (something may happen during the flight), and wary about relationships (he may lose a loved one).

Why? What is it precisely that is paralysing him? It is not primarily the prospect of getting bad news or suffering harm, but the despair-inducing suspicion that whatever harm he suffers will be his undoing. In other words, it is not primarily the possibility of trials but the significance of possible trials that haunts him. Some good may ultimately come of his struggles, he admits, but that potential good seems so small next to the possible pain. The dreadful things that might happen to him—those now loom so large that all other considerations (especially God's good purposes) are blocked from sight.

POUTING

The third challenge I have encountered as a cancer survivor is the temptation, in dark moments, to wish that I had not survived.

That sounds foolish, I know, but is sinful ingratitude not the height of folly?

In moments of difficulty and frustration you can find yourself muttering (at least in your heart), 'It would have been better if cancer had taken my life. Then I wouldn't have to put up with all of this. Then I'd be free.' You may even go on to mutter, 'What was God thinking, letting me live the way that he did? Why didn't he just let me die? Couldn't he see that it would have been better?'

To make matters worse, we can tell ourselves that we are being holy to wish and wonder such things. 'See how holy I am, that I wish I were in heaven right now, free from sin.' Yes, it is holy to long for the sinlessness of heaven. But no, it is not holy to charge that God failed you when he did not take you there as soon as possible.

This is the grown-up version (though, strictly speaking, it reflects little growth) of the pouting we sometimes see on children's faces. Have you ever seen a child who has been given a gift but then experiences frustration in the use of it? Picture the little boy who throws his new baseball glove to the ground in disgust because he finds that the ball does not automatically find its way into the glove every time. 'Stupid glove!' Then picture the little boy's father who casts his new golf club into the lake, cursing the golf gods as he does so, because his approach shot just went into that same lake. 'Stupid club!' Like father, like son. Well, when someone who has survived a serious illness runs into obstacles and disappointments later in life, he is tempted to mutter, 'Stupid life! Wouldn't death have been better?'

If such language has a familiar ring to it, that may be because we hear it in the Bible, especially in the Old Testament. Remember how the people of Israel responded when they found themselves caught between the Red Sea before them and the army of Egypt behind them:

> They said to Moses, 'Is it because there are no graves in Egypt that you have taken us away to die in the wilderness? What have you done to us in bringing us out of Egypt? Is not this what we said to you in Egypt: "Leave us alone that we may serve the Egyptians"? For it would have been better for us to serve the Egyptians than to die in the wilderness' (*Exod.* 14:11–12).

When the going got tough, Israel pouted. They did it again in Exodus 16. And then they did it again in Exodus 17. And then they did it again in Numbers 14.

Notice Israel's charge: 'It would have been better for us to serve the Egyptians.' It was against Moses that they levelled that charge, but remember that Israel's grumbling against Moses amounted to grumbling against God himself, because Moses was serving as God's specially appointed representative. Moses himself makes that plain in Exodus 16:6–8. He said to Israel, 'Your grumbling is not against us [that is, against Moses and Aaron] but against the LORD.' Thus Israel's charge amounted to this: 'God, you failed to do what was better. You acted foolishly when you brought us out of Egypt. What were you thinking?' In short, the Lord had preserved them, and Israel's response was to allege that he had been foolish to do so. And they made that allegation over and over again.

KNOWING GOD
Presumption. Paralysis. Pouting.

Every Christian, not only the cancer survivor, needs to be wary of those three. After all, every Christian still wrestles with pride and unbelief in his own heart as he lives in a world of trial and uncertainty.

Now, notice that each of those three 'P's amounts in its own way to a failure to know God.

First, when we presume upon the future we show that we do not know well the sovereignty of God. We have lost sight of the fact that he is still in charge and thus still perfectly free to depart from any script we may have written for him. In our imagination we have demoted him, either turning him into our partner in the management of our lives, or, worse, relegating him to the position of our subordinate.

Second, when we who are in Christ find ourselves paralysed with fear we reveal that we have not come to grips with the goodness of God. We struggle to believe that he brings trials into our lives in order to bring about a final blessedness for us that vastly outweighs them. Contrary to Jesus' teaching (*Matt.* 7:9–10), we have imagined God to be like a father who gives to his needy children stones and serpents instead of bread and fish.

Third, when we pout about our blessings we betray that we do not thoroughly trust in the wisdom of God. In our minds we have made him out to be a god who does not know what he is doing, misguided in his attempts to do us good. He may be well-intentioned, but his good intentions sometimes lead him to blunder. 'Thanks, God, but you shouldn't have. I mean, you really shouldn't have.'

You see, in each case we have imagined God to be something other than what he has actually revealed himself to be. We have turned him into a different god altogether. In effect, we have invented a new god in our minds that has taken the place of the biblical God.

Now, stop and consider the alternative god that we have constructed here. He is a god:

(1.) who is not in ultimate control,

(2.) who is sometimes cruel, and

(3.) who is sometimes foolish.

Does that sound familiar? If so, that is because it sounds just like us! We are not in ultimate control, and are sometimes cruel, and are sometimes foolish. Lo and behold, we have managed to make a god after our own image. And having done so, is it any wonder that we will relate to him in the ways we have been considering? You see, we are prone to lapse into presumption, paralysis or pouting (or into a host of other spiritual ills, for that matter) when we start thinking that God is little better than a big, invisible man, all too much like the men that we see, like the men that we are. As Martin Luther famously remarked to Desiderius Erasmus, 'Your thoughts about God are all too human.'[1] Two very different biblical spokes-

---

[1] Martin Luther, *The Bondage of the Will*, tr. Philip S. Watson and Benjamin Drewery, in *Luther's Works*, vol. 33, *Career of the Reformer III* (Philadelphia: Fortress Press, 1972), p. 47.

men (Balaam in *Num.* 23:19 and Samuel in *1 Sam.* 15:29) teach us this important lesson: God is not a man, and thus he does not act like one. The Lord himself teaches the same lesson in the form of a thundering rhetorical question: 'To whom then will you compare me, that I should be like him? says the Holy One' (*Isa.* 40:25). J. I. Packer, in his *Knowing God*, reflects upon that question in Isaiah 40 and challenges us accordingly:

> Our thoughts of God are not great enough; we fail to reckon with the reality of His limitless wisdom and power. Because we ourselves are limited and weak, we imagine that at some points God is too, and find it hard to believe that He is not. We think of God as too much like what we are. Put this mistake right, says God; learn to acknowledge the full majesty of your incomparable God and Saviour.[2]

So then, let us return to our God and know him afresh.

Let us know that our God is still sovereign, and thus put presumption to death. We do not reign. The Lord reigns. And he does so every moment, all our lives. He reigns before, during and after every trial and every blessing. He owes no man a 'happily ever after' of health and wealth, peace and prosperity, in this life. Go back and meditate again upon those 'spectrum texts' in Chapter 2. They are still true here in Chapter 9!

Let us know that our God is good, and thus free ourselves from paralysing fear. 'And we know that for those who love God all things work together for good, for those who are called according to his purpose' (*Rom.* 8:28). For the Christian the goodness of God is no abstraction. The Christian believes not only that God is good; he believes also that God is good toward him. He takes God's goodness personally. He trusts that God loves him so as to

[2] J. I. Packer, *Knowing God* (Downers Grove, Illinois: InterVarsity, 1973), pp. 78–9.

save him. 'For you, O Lord, are good and forgiving, abounding in steadfast love to all who call upon you' (*Psa.* 86:5).

So may we trust and live today. Instead of allowing possible pain to loom so large in our minds that it blocks everything else from sight, let us embrace the Bible's very different sense of perspective: 'For this light momentary affliction is preparing for us an eternal weight of glory beyond all comparison' (*2 Cor.* 4:17); 'For I consider that the sufferings of this present time are not worth comparing with the glory that is to be revealed to us' (*Rom.* 8:18). Do you see in those passages the Apostle Paul's perspective? We tend to see present sufferings as large and future glory as small, but for Paul it is the reverse! Here is the goodness of God: yes, he brings us pains, but he does so in order to bring us into conformity to Christ and finally to bring us home. Beyond all comparison, indeed.

Grasping the goodness of God in this way is a key that unlocks the shackle of paralysing fear. Psalm 112 pronounces, 'Blessed is the man who fears the LORD' (verse 1), and then it describes that man in these terms: 'He is not afraid of bad news; his heart is firm, trusting in the LORD' (verse 7). Not afraid! A friend in our congregation shared that Bible verse with me early on in our ordeal, and I am glad he did. Notice, it is not that the God-fearing man never receives bad news. Rather, it is that he trusts firmly in the goodness of the One who is behind all news. That is why he does not live in cowering fear of what might be around the next bend in the road. Whatever it turns out to be, he trusts that his good God will have placed it there.

One who grasped this—and preached this—was the nineteenth-century Presbyterian pastor and theologian, Robert L. Dabney. In a sermon entitled 'True Courage,' Dabney acknowledged that the Christian is just as susceptible to the dangers of life as any man, but it is his faith in the goodness of God (plus the sovereignty and wisdom of God, by the way) that sets him free and makes him truly courageous:

> Now, the child of God is not taught what is the special will of God as to himself; he has no revelation as to the security of his person. Nor does he presume to predict what particular dispensation God will grant to the cause in which he is embarked. But he knows that, be it what it may, it will be wise, and right, and good. Whether the arrows of death shall smite him or pass him by, he knows no more than the unbelieving sinner; but he knows that neither event can happen to him without the purpose and will of his Heavenly Father. And that will, be it whichever it may, is guided by divine wisdom and love. Should the event prove a revelation of God's decision, and this was the place, and this the hour, for life to end; then he accepts it with calm submission; for are not the time and place chosen for him by the All-wise, who loves him from eternity? Him who walks in the true fear of God, God loves.[3]

In that conviction lies the source of true courage. As Dabney went on to say:

> In proportion as God's children have faith to embrace the love of God to them, are they lifted in spirit to his very throne, and can look down upon the rage of battle, and the tumult of the people, with some of the holy disdain, the ineffable security, which constitute the blessedness of God.[4]

Finally, let us know that our God is wise, and thus leave our pouting behind. Did God bless you in some way in the past? He knew what he was doing. Has that very blessing led to the experience of new frustrations in the present (like that little boy's

---

[3] Robert L. Dabney, 'True Courage', in *Discussions*, ed. C. R. Vaughan, vol. 4, (Harrisonburg, Virginia: Sprinkle Publications, 1994), p. 441.

[4] Dabney, *Discussions* vol. 4, p. 442.

baseball glove)? God still knows what he is doing. Do not second-guess him. A day is coming (that heavenly Day) when you will see just how wise he was all along.

If you are reading this, I know this much: God has been pleased to preserve your life, whether you have ever had a serious illness or not. After all, every breath that any of us draws is a gift from him. If you ever feel yourself tempted to mutter 'Stupid life!' in a moment of disappointment or frustration, remember: the life you are tempted to curse is the one that the All-wise thought it best to give you. 'Oh, the depth of the riches and wisdom and knowledge of God! How unsearchable are his judgments and how inscrutable his ways! "For who has known the mind of the Lord, or who has been his counsellor?"' (*Rom.* 11:33–34). So, will you counsel God, or will you trust in him? Let us trust.

'AND SO TO HIM I LEAVE IT ALL'

Remember the hymn with which we began, 'Whate'er My God Ordains Is Right.' The first verse ends with these words, 'Wherefore to him I leave it all', and the fourth and final verse concludes similarly: 'And so to him I leave it all.' This, then, is a recurring refrain in the hymn. The question is, have we made it the refrain of our lives?

What does it mean to leave all things to God? First, consider what it does not mean. Obviously, it does not mean giving our trials back to God so that we do not have to deal with them any more, as if we could box them up and leave them in a package on our front porch marked 'Return to Sender'. We have no such power. Close your eyes and tap your heels together three times and say to yourself, 'And so to him I leave it all' . . . and you will find when you open your eyes that the box is still sitting there. 'But God, I left my trials to you. Why are they still here? Why didn't you pick up the package?' No, there is no such delivery option.

More seriously, leaving all things to God does not mean switching into a mode of passivity. The Christian life is just that—it is a life, not a slumber. These trials that we cannot give back to God in a box, he has given them to us as a calling. We must not sit back and expect him to make the most of them without any engagement on our part. Remember Paul's striking statement in Philippians 2: 'work out your own salvation with fear and trembling, for it is God who works in you, both to will and to work for his good pleasure' (verses 12–13). The implication is that God normally makes the most of the trials in our lives by stirring us to make the most of them and by dealing graciously with us as we do so. And we make the most of them as we are actively engaged: everything from spiritual reflection to practical problem-solving. See? No passivity here.

So then, put positively, what does it mean to leave all things to God? In short, it means resting in the very truths we have considered in this chapter: God's sovereignty, God's goodness, God's wisdom. It means admitting our own powerlessness to figure everything out and to fix everything that is broken, and then trusting that our God is not stymied as we are. You see, there is rest for the weary after all! No, it is not the rest of inactivity, but something far better: the peace of heart that comes from knowing that there is such a God, and that he is our God, and we are his people. Just days after I was diagnosed I was given a framed print of the words of Isaiah 26:3, and it still hangs on the wall in my study: 'Thou wilt keep him in perfect peace, whose mind is stayed on thee' (AV). God is the Alpha, the one who has ordained our circumstances, and he is the Omega, the one who will guide us to his glory. His are the details. His are the outcomes. Will you stay your mind on him? Will you leave all things to him?

PRESSING ON

I said at the outset of this book that my aim in writing it was to share lessons 'learned'—past tense—during our cancer experience. Yes, Christy and I learned these things all those years ago, but of course we have been re-learning them ever since, and we will be doing so until we reach the end. The Christian life is like that. It is a life of regularly re-covering truths already covered and applied. After all, we sinners are a forgetful lot, needy of periodic reminders, plus we are constantly confronting new circumstances in which familiar truths must be brought to bear in not-so-familiar ways. Walking a dark road for a while does not have the effect of automatically raising you to a higher spiritual plane where all the lessons have been fully learned. After all, to be a 'disciple' is to be a learner in Christ's school, and we are still disciples, still walking with our Teacher and listening to him as he leads us down this road that keeps going.

How dark, or bright, is your road now? More importantly, how is your heart? Is it dark with the shadows of discouragement and loneliness, or is it bright with the love of God and the hope of heaven? In measure every Christian knows both darkness and light, until he reaches that land where 'night will be no more' (*Rev.* 22:5).

Do you find some of that darkness within? Then before you close this book and set it down, go back to the Preface and read the words of Samuel Rodigast's poem, 'Whate'er My God Ordains Is Right', one more time. Those words are true. My God is true. May you walk with him as your God, too.